ULTIMATE BATHROOM Book

Not One Of Your Uncles Bathroom Readers.

Farrell Kingsley

Ultimate Bathroom Book

ISBN-13:
978-0615427980 (Orchid Press Publishing)

ISBN-10:
0615427987

This book is dedicated to:

All those at Orchid Press Publishing who had the faith in me to complete this project.

INDEX

MEN AND WOMEN 96

THE BEST OF CRAIGLIST.COM FOR 2009-2010 146

FUN FACTS 196

How Al Capone Was Tied To The First Fighter Ace of WWII

Al Capone is America's best known for many things such as his stint in the Federal Alcatraz Prison and also as being one of the 1920's and 30's worst and most violent mobsters in Chicago. Capone had a leading mans role in the illegal activities that earned Chicago a reputation as being a lawless city.

Al Capone's mug shot from a 1931 arrest.

Alphonsus Capone was born on January 17, 1899, in Brooklyn, New York. Before he was ten he became a member of two "kid gangs," the Brooklyn Rippers and the Forty Thieves Juniors. Capone quit school during his sixth grade year around the age of fourteen. He ran some scams but also held down some odd jobs such as being a clerk in a candy store, he was also a pin boy in a bowling alley, and gained skills as a cutter in a book bindery.

He next became a member of the notorious Five Points gang in Manhattan and worked in gangster Frankie Yale's Brooklyn dive, the Harvard Inn. His short but muscular build lent him to be a bouncer and a part-time bartender. During a fight in the bar, Capone received cuts on his face and soon after he got the nickname "Scarface". The rumor was that Capone insulted a female patron whose brother came back for revenge.

Sometime early in the year of 1918, Capone met an Irish girl named Mary "Mae" Coughlin and asked her to dance. On December 4, 1918, Mae gave birth to Capone's son which the couple named, Albert "Sonny" Francis. Capone and Mae were married on December 30, 1918.

Capone's very first arrest was for disorderly conduct while he was working for the gangster Frankie Yale. Many believe that Capone also murdered two men while in New York. However, no one ever admitted to hearing or seeing a thing so we will never know for sure and Capone was never tried for the murders.

Soon after that Capone hospitalized a rival gang member and Yale sent him to Chicago to wait until things cooled off for his safety. Capone arrived in Chicago in 1919 and moved his family into a house at 7244 South Prairie Avenue.

Capone's first home at 7244 South Prairie Avenue.

Yale got Capone a job working for outlaw John Torrio. Torrio immediately saw Capone's potential and encouraged Capone to be his protégé. Soon Capone was learning all of the facets of Torrio's bootlegging business.

Sometime in the middle of 1922 Torrio named Capone as his right hand man or "number two man" and eventually the two became full partners in many business enterprises such as saloons, gambling houses, and brothels.

By 1924, Torrio had been shot by rival gang members and consequently decided to leave the Chicago area. Capone inherited the entire organization and made sure everyone knew who was the boss. Most of Capone's henchmen were loyal and called Capone the "The Big Fellow."

He soon proved to all of his associates and rivals that he was even better at running the organization than Torrio. Capone syndicated and expanded the city's bootlegging, gambling houses, and the sin industry between 1925 and 1930.

Capone controlled speakeasies, bookie joints, gambling houses, brothels, horse and race tracks, nightclubs, distilleries and breweries at a reported income of over one hundred million dollars a year. He even acquired a sizable interest in the largest cleaning and dyeing plant chain in Chicago.

There were many attempts on Capone's life over the years but none were ever successful. Capone setup an extensive spy network in Chicago, from newspaper boys to policemen. Any plots to hurt Capone were quickly discovered and dwelt with severely.

Capone was great at killing his enemies when they became too powerful. A typical Capone murder consisted of hit-men renting an apartment across the street from the victim's residence. When the victim stepped out in the open, death became sudden and swift with Capone always having an unshakable alibi.

Although Capone ordered dozens of his rival's deaths, he often treated people fairly and generously. When the stock market crashed in 1929 he was quick to open soup kitchens and he ordered merchants to give clothes and food to the needy which Capone quickly paid for.

A 1929 soup kitchen organized by Capone.

Capone was never tried for most of his crimes. He was arrested in 1926 for killing three people, but spent only one night in jail because there was insufficient evidence to connect him with the murders and he had an Ace in his corner. A young lawyer going by the name of Easy Eddie who was very good. In fact, because of his skill, he was able to keep Al Capone out of jail on many occasions.

Capone talking to his lawyer Easy Eddie.

To show his appreciation to Easy Eddie, Al Capone paid him very well. He not only earned big money, Capone bought him a residence that filled an entire Chicago City block and fenced it in. To add to that Capone paid live-in help and furnished the house with all of the conveniences of the time period.

Easy Eddie had a son and gave him all the best things money could buy. While he was growing up he had the nicest clothes, cars, and a good education. He sheltered his son from the life he lived and he tried to teach him right from wrong.

Although Easy Eddie was sheltered from prosecution by being Capone's lawyer something convinced Easy Eddie to talk to the authorities and right some of the wrongs he knew about.

He decided to go to authorities and testify against Al Capone. Eddie knew that Al Capone would do his best to have him killed. And within the year Al Capone had done exactly that. Easy Eddie was shot and killed on a street in Chicago.

Eventually Al Capone was convicted of tax evasion and went on to serve time in prison including the Federal Prison Alcatraz. When he was released he soon died of complications of a stroke and dementia brought on by Syphilis.

During World War II, many people gained fame in one way or another. One man was Butch O'Hare. He was a fighter pilot assigned to an aircraft carrier in the Pacific. During one of the first missions of the war his entire squadron was assigned to fly a mission. As soon as Butch was airborne, he looked at his fuel gauge and realized that someone had forgotten to fill up his fuel tank.

There was no way he would not have enough fuel to complete his mission and he left the flight squadron and headed back to the carrier after the flight leader told him to leave formation.

On his way back to the carrier he could see a squadron of Japanese Zeroes scanning the waters for the carrier and planning to attack if they found it. Butch knew that all the fighter cover was gone on the mission. He knew with all the fighter planes gone, the fleet was almost defenseless. Knowing almost surely he would die, he knew he had the only opportunity to distract and divert the Japanese Zeros.

He dove straight down through the middle of the formation of Japanese planes and attacked them shooting one down almost instantly as he went down. Butch's fighter plane was one of the planes which had been rigged with cameras, so that as he flew and fought, pictures would be taken so pilots could learn more about the terrain, enemy maneuvers, and other information.

Butch dove at the Zeros and shot at them shooting down four more planes. And when his ammunition was gone, he started flying crazily and clipping off wing after wing and several tails. He targeted anything that would make the enemy planes unfit to fly.

In such close quarters the Japanese planes were defenseless and chose safety over trying to shoot the crazy American flyer down and accidentally hitting their own places. The Japanese flyers decided to avoid the crazy American fighter at all costs and changed direction not knowing that just in a few more miles they would have discovered the American carrier and the rest of the American fleet.

Although Butch O'Hare and his fighter were badly shot up, he limped his plane back to the carrier. He told his story but not one of his superiors believed him until someone mentioned the camera he had on board his plane. That is where the truth was revealed.

It wasn't until the film from the camera on his plane was developed, did everyone realize the extent Butch O'Hare went to protect his carrier and the entire fleet. He was immediately recognized as a hero and given one of the nation's highest military honors for bravery.

Sadly less than a year later, Butch O'Hare was shot down and killed during the war. But he was not forgotten. Chicago named their airport after one of their own. They named the airport after the very first Fighter Ace of World War II calling it the Butch O'Hare Airport. Which is now one of the busiest airports in the world.

You may know the airport in Chicago as simply "O'Hare" or "O'Hare Airport".

Butch O'Hare in his plane showing the five kills which made him the first Fighter Ace of WWII.

Now through the last few pages you may be wondering how a story about Butch O'Hare fits in to a story about Al Capone and Easy Eddie. They sound like two unrelated stories in two completely different time periods. Do you remember the small boy who Easy Eddie kept from the crime ridden world that he lived in and gave the best education to?

Easy Eddie's real name was Edward J. O'Hare and Butch O'Hare was his son.

All About the Great Depression

America's "Great Depression" began with the dramatic crash of the stock market which was called "Black Thursday" on October 24, 1929. On that day over 16 million shares of stock were quickly sold by panicking investors who had suddenly lost faith in the American economy. At the height of the Depression in 1933, nearly 25% of the Nation's total work force, 12,830,000 people, were unemployed.

The income for workers who were lucky enough to have kept their jobs fell more than 40% between 1929 and 1933. It was the worst economic disaster in American history. Farm prices fell so much that many farmers lost their homes and land.

Many went hungry during the depression. All over the U.S. there were small towns constructed of packing crates, abandoned cars and other cast off scraps sprung up across the Nation. Gangs of youths, whose families could no longer support them, rode the rails in box cars like so many hoboes, hoping to find a job. "

America's unemployed to move to get better work. Sometimes moving just based on rumors they heard. There was really nowhere to go. Every industry was badly shaken by the depression. Factories closed; mills and mines were abandoned; fortunes were lost.

Unable to help themselves, the American public looked to the Federal Government for help. Dissatisfied with President Herbert Hoover's economic programs, the people elected Franklin D. Roosevelt as their president in 1932. Early in Roosevelt's administration he assembled the best minds possible in the country to advise him. This group of men were known as the "Brain Trust." Within one hundred days the President, his advisors and the U.S. Congress passed into law a package of legislation designed to help lift the out of the depression.

Roosevelt's program called his program the "New Deal." The words "New Deal" signified a new relationship between the American people and the U.S. government.

Part of the package was to have the government take on many new responsibilities for the welfare of the people. The new relationship forged in the New Deal program was one of closeness between the government and the people: a closeness which had never existed to such a degree before.

Despite all of Franklin's efforts and the courage of the American people, the Depression hung on until 1941, when America's involvement in the Second World War resulted in the drafting of young men into military service, and the creation of millions of jobs in defense and war industries.

Facts of The Great Depression

1. On "Black Tuesday," October 29, 1929, the market lost $14 billion, making the loss for that week an astounding $30 billion. This was ten times more than the annual federal budget. Thirty billion dollars in 1929 would be equivalent to $400,000,000,000 today.

2. Herbert Hoover (1874-1964), a Republican, was president when the Great Depression began. He declared in March 1930 that the U.S. had "passed the worst" and argued that the economy would sort itself out.

3. Chicago gangster Al Capone (1899-1947) as we learned in the last section made sporadic attempts at public relations by opening a soup kitchen during the Great Depression.

4. Shortly after the crash in 1929, there was a wave of suicides in the New York's financial district. Clerks in some hotels even started asking new guests if they needed a room for sleeping or jumping.

5. The Great Depression is widely believed to have been the result of a weak banking system, overproduction of industry, a bursting credit bubble, and a lack of profit sharing between farmers and industrial workers in the

1920s.

6. In response to the economic crisis, designers created more affordable fashions with longer hemlines, slim waistlines, lower heels, and less makeup for women.

7. During the worst years of the Depression (1933-1934) the overall jobless rate was 25% (1 out of 4 people) with another 25% taking wage cuts or working part time.

8. The gross national product fell by almost 50% during the Depression.

9. It took a world war in 1941, to get the unemployment rate officially below 10%.

10. Scholars estimate that over 50% of children during the Depression did not have adequate food, shelter, or medical care.

11. There were some very famous people who would ride on railroad cars because they didn't have money to travel. Some famous men who rode the rails were:
    *   William O. Douglas (1898-1980)
    *   U.S. Supreme Court Justice from(1939-1975)
    *   Novelist Louis L'Amour (1908-1988)
    *   Folk singer Woody Guthrie (1912-1967).

12. The board game Monopoly, was a result of the depression and was first sold in 1935.

13. It is estimated that more than 50,000 people were injured or killed while jumping trains trying to ride them during the Depression.

14. Disney released the "Three Little Pigs"in 1933. It was largely seen as symbolic of the Great Depression, with the wolf representing the Depression. The three little pigs represented the average citizens.

15. During the Great Depression there were also several popular movies released. Those were *The Wizard of Oz* (1939) and *Gone with the Wind* (1939).

16. African-Americans seemed to be the hardest hit during the Great Depression, and they were often the first to get laid off and the last to get hired.

17. During the Depression, distressed farms were sometimes sold at "Penny Auction" (forced auctions) in which farmers

would assure that a distressed neighbor would be able to buy back his own farm by holding bids down to pennies, nickels, and quarters. Over 750,000 farms were sold at these auctions.

18. A number of giant structures, including the Empire State Building and the Golden Gate Bridge, were completed during the Great Depression, to help provide jobs to the unemployed.

19. In some mountain communities people survived only by eating dandelions and blackberries for their basic diet.

20. During the Depression children were so hungry; they chewed on their own hands.

21. As businesses and farms closed during the Great Depression created a large number of criminals such as:
    1. John Dillinger
    2. Lester M. Gillis ("Baby Face" Nelson)
    3. Machine Gun Kelly
    4. Pretty Boy Floyd
    5. Ma Barker and her Boys
    6. Bonnie and Clyde

22. As news of the stock market crash spread, customers rushed to their banks to withdraw all their money creating bank failures as many deposits were used as loans to their customers.

23. Milton Friedman a noted economist argues that the 1930s market crash itself did not cause the depression, but rather it was the collapse of the banking system during waves of public panic during 1930-1933.

24. Social Security began in 1935, to guarantee money for the elderly who did not have enough money to support themselves.

25. In the 1930s, thousands of schools were operating on reduced hours or were closed down completely. Some three million children had left school and over 60 percent of the teachers had lost jobs.

26. In New York City it was estimated that there were as many as 6,000 apple sellers each day to avoid panhandling.

27. Mexican-Americans were accused of taking jobs away from

"real" Americans. Some American drove them from towns and accused them of unfairly burdening local relief efforts.

28. In 1929, Soviet leader Joseph Stalin told a small group of American communists that America would experience a revolutionary crisis. He told them to be ready to assume the leadership of America during the "impending class struggle in America."

29. During the Great Depression women were also accused of taking away jobs from men and driven from some types of jobs.

30. During Great Depression many couples delayed marriage, divorce rates dropped, and birth rates declined.

31. A 1940 poll revealed that 1.5 million married women were abandoned by their husbands during the great depression because they couldn't provide for them and themselves.

32. Severe drought and dust storms turned bad in to worse as it dried out farmlands and forced families to leave their farms. In one storm alone that came on May 9, 1934, an estimated 350 million tons of dirt was carried 2,000 miles east ward to Chicago killing tens of thousands of animals.

33. In Cleveland, Ohio, over 50% of the population was jobless.

34. In 1936, main economic indicators (except unemployment) regained the levels of the late 1920s...but after the federal government cut spending with the expectation that the private sector would step in, the economy took another sharp downturn until WWII.

35. Californians tried to stop migrants from moving into their state by creating checkpoints on main highways called "bum blockades." California even instated an "anti-Okie" law which punished anyone bringing in "indigents" with jail time.

36. During the Great Depression, hundreds of thousands of families traveled west on Route 66 to California, following what John Steinbeck in his famous novel *The Grapes of Wrath* called "The Mother Road."

37. While John Steinbeck highlights the plight of migrant farm families in *The Grapes of Wrath*, in reality, less than half (43%)

of the migrants were farmers. Most migrants came from east of the Dust Bowl and did not work on farms.

38. Every major country, including the United States, abandoned the gold standard during the Great Depression. In fact, leaving the gold standard was a predictor of a country's economic severity and the length of time for its recovery. However, Herbert Hoover argued that abandoning the gold standard was the first step toward "communism, fascism, socialism, statism, and a planned economy."

39. As he did during WWII, Joseph P. Kennedy (JFK's father) amassed an enormous amount of wealth through real estate (among other ventures) during the Great Depression. Without this money, he could not have financed his son's successful run for the presidency.

Gas Prices Really Expensive?

Do you really think that gas is expensive a little around $3.00 per gallon? Let's take a look at some other common liquid items and let's see what they would be if we bought them by the gallon. This kind of puts things in perspective.

Slurpee 16 oz $1.29 .... $10.32 per gallon

Lipton Ice Tea 16 oz $1.19 .... $9.52 per gallon

Gatorade 20 oz $1.59 .... $10.17 per gallon

Ocean Spray 16 oz $1.25 .... $10.00 per gallon

Movie Theatre Soda 16oz $5.00.. $40.00 per gallon

Brake Fluid 12 oz $3.15 .... $33.60 per gallon

Vick's Nyquil 6 oz $8.35 .... $178.13 per gallon

Pepto Bismol 4 oz $3.85 .... $123.20 per gallon

Whiteout 7 oz $1.39 .... $25.42 per gallon

Scope 1.5 oz $0.99 .... $84.48 per gallon

Evian water 9 oz $1.49 .... $21.19 per gallon

InkJet Printer Ink .... $4,900.00 per gallon

So, the next time you're at the pump, be glad your car doesn't run on printer ink.

Real Comments from Government Employee Reviews

If you have ever had an employee evaluation at your job, you might not understand that they could have been worse even if you had a bad one. These are actual quotes taken from Federal Government employee performance evaluations:

1. "Since my last report, this employee has reached rock-bottom and has started to dig."

2. "I would not allow this employee to breed."

3. "This employee is really not so much of a has-been, but more of a definite won't be."

4. "Works well when under constant supervision and cornered like a rat in a trap."

5. "When she opens her mouth, it seems that it is only to change feet."

6. "This young lady has delusions of adequacy."

7. "He sets low personal standards and then consistently fails to achieve them."

8. "This employee is depriving a village somewhere of an idiot."

9. "This employee should go far, and the sooner he starts, the better."

10. "Got a full 6-pack, but lacks the plastic thingy to hold it all together."

11. "A gross ignoramus -- 144 times worse than an ordinary ignoramus."

12. "He doesn't have ulcers, but he's a carrier."

13. "He's been working with glue too much."

14. "He would argue with a signpost."

15. "He brings a lot of joy whenever he leaves the room."

16. "When his IQ reaches 50, he should sell."

17. "Some drink from the fountain of knowledge; he only gargled."

18. "Takes him 2 hours to watch '60-minutes'."

19. "If you see two people talking and one looks bored, he's the other one."

20. "A photographic memory but with the lens cover glued on."

21. "A prime candidate for natural de-selection."

22. "Donated his brain to science before he was done using it."

23. "Gates are down, the lights are flashing, but the train isn't coming."

24. "He's got two brains cells, one is lost and the other is out looking for it."

25. "If he were any more stupid, he'd have to be watered twice a week."

26. "If you give him a penny for his thoughts, you'd get change."

27. "If you stand close enough to him, you can hear the ocean."

28. "It's hard to believe he beat out 1,000,000 other sperm."

29. "One neuron short of a synapse."

30. "The wheel is turning, but the hamster is dead.

Saturn's Interesting Facts

1. The moon Titan which circles Saturn has an atmosphere similar to earths.

2. Conditions on Titan may resemble ancient Earth conditions, though at a much lower temperature.

3. A year on Earth is 365 days. A year on Saturn is 10,759 days.

4. Approximately 750 Earths could fit inside of Saturn.

5. A day on Earth is 24 hours. A day on Saturn is 10 hours 39 minutes.

6. Saturn is the second-largest planet in our solar system. Only Jupiter is larger.

7. Jupiter, Uranus, and Neptune also have rings just like Saturn's.

8. Saturn is the least dense planet in the solar system, and if there were a body of water large enough to hold Saturn, the planet would float. In contrast, Earth and Mercury would sink the fastest.

9. It takes about 29.5 Earth years for Saturn to orbit around our sun.

10. Launched on October 15, 1997, the Cassini-Huygens spacecraft traveled over 2,000,000,000 miles at a speed of 70,700 miles per hour before it reached the ringed planet in 2004.

11. The first spacecraft to fly by Saturn was Pioneer 11, which blasted off in 1973 and arrived at Saturn in 1979.

12. Voyagers 1 and 2 also completed fly-bys of Saturn in 1980 and 1981. (Voyager 1 is now the farthest human-made object in space.)

13. Saturn is 74,898 miles (120,537 km.) wide, nearly 10 times wider than Earth which is the 5th largest planet.

14. Nearly 1,600 Saturn's could fit inside the Sun.

15. Saturn's moon Titan is the second-largest moon in the solar system. Only Jupiter's moon Ganymede is larger.

16. The moon Titan is bigger than the planet Mercury.

17. Winds in Saturn's atmosphere travel up to 1,100 miles. Even the strongest tornadoes on Earth have ever reached speeds of only about 300 miles per hour.

18. Storms on Saturn can last for months or even years.

19. As the seventh day of the week, Saturday is named after Saturn.

20. Saturn rotates at about 6,200 miles per hour. It rotates so fast that the planet bulges at its equator and its poles are flat.

21. Discovered in 1789 by William Herschel, Saturn's moon Enceladus has geysers that erupt with icy particles, water vapor, and organic compounds.

22. The moon Enceladus is the shiniest object in the solar system because of its icy surface reflects most of the light it receives.

23. Saturn's weather is determined by conditions deep in the planet rather than by the Sun.

24. Summer on Saturn lasts about eight Earth years.

25. The planet's core is a ball of rock, about the size of Earth.

26. The atmospheric pressure on Saturn is over 90 times greater than the Earth's atmospheric pressure. The pressure is so great that it even gas molecules into liquid. If we tried to land a spacecraft on Saturn It would be crushed before it hit the ground.

27. The temperature at Saturn's core is estimated to be about 21,150° F, which is about as hot as the surface of the Sun.

28. Lightening is common on Saturn, though the bolts run only from cloud to cloud, unlike the cloud-to-ground lightening on Earth.

29. Saturn's rings are only a few hundred feet thick, which is less than half the length of a football field. Mainly made up of lose rock, ice and meteorites. Some as small as a grain of sand and others about the size of a house.

30. Saturn has 61 moons.

31. Earth receives about 90 times more sunlight than Saturn.

32. Saturn's diameter is estimated to be around 74,580 miles.

33. Every fourteen years Saturn's rings seem to disappear. Scientists believe that the rings may disappear when Saturn is tilted directly in line with Earth.

Scared Of Sharks?

1. Approximately 100 million sharks are killed every year. Most are killed to make shake teeth necklaces, fertilizers, soups, leather from their skin, and to get the oil from their liver which is used to make vitamins, face cream, soap, and fuel.

2. Before dinosaurs roamed the earth, sharks hunted through the oceans.

3. Sharks belong to a group of fish known as the *elasmobranches*, or cartilaginous fishes.

4. Sharks very rarely get cancer enabling scientists study their cartilage in the hopes of finding a cure for the disease.

5. Sharks have the most powerful jaws on the planet. Both the sharks' upper and lower jaws move.

6. A shark bites with its lower jaw first and then its upper. It tosses its head back and forth to tear loose pieces of meat which it swallows whole.

7. Hammerhead sharks' heads are soft at birth so they won't jam the mothers' birth canals.

8. The first written account of a shark attack is found in Herodotus' (c. 484–425 B.C.) which described hordes of "monsters" devouring the shipwrecked sailors of a Persian fleet.

9. When a shark eats food that it can't digest (like a turtle shell or tin can), it can vomit by thrusting its stomach out its mouth then pulling it right back in. Ooh.

10. Scientists suggest women stay out of the water while menstruating as sharks can detect a single drop of blood in the water up to a mile away.

11. Shark skin was used as sandpaper called *Shagreen*, to smooth and polish wood.

12. The first pup to hatch inside the sand tiger shark mother eats its brothers and sisters sometimes leaving only two pups, one on each side of the womb. This form of cannibalism is called *oophagy*.

13. Each type of shark has a different shaped tooth depending on its diet

14. Sharks have 40-45 teeth, with up to seven rows of replacement teeth behind them.

15. When a shark breaks or loses a tooth in the front of its mouth, it only takes about a day for a replacement tooth to move forward to the front row.

16. The longest shark in the world is the whale shark, which can grow to a whopping 50 feet long and weigh more than 40,000 pounds.

17. Nearly 90% of shark attacks have happened to men.

18. Many out of place items have been found in shark stomachs such as anchors, shoes, silverware, chairs, half of a horse, a box of nails, a torpedo, drum, a car tire, and bottles of wine.

19. Most sharks are completely harmless.

20. Sharks do not have a single bone in their bodies.

21. Japanese warriors wrapped shark skin around the handles of their swords to keep the swords from slipping out of their hands.

22. The Grey Reef shark (Carcharhinus amblyrhynchos) has been called the "gangster shark" and is highly aggressive nature.

23. Typical sharks can go through more than 30,000 teeth in a lifetime. Newer teeth are always larger than the last.

24. Two-thirds of a shark's brain is dedicated to its super sense of smell

25. The frilled shark, or eel shark, is called a "living fossil" because it is so much like some extinct sharks that are found preserved in rocks.

26. Portuguese sharks can live at depths of over two miles deep.

27. A nine-foot-long bull shark can swim in just two feet of water.

28. Almost all sharks are "carnivores" or meat eaters.

29. Most sharks live on a diet of fish and sea mammals such as dolphins, seals, turtles and sometimes seagulls.

30. Most shark attacks occur less than 100 feet from the shore.

31. Shark attacks happen all over the world, but mainly around popular beaches in North America.

32. Worldwide about 30 people die each year from shark attacks.

33. Sharks will often give warning signs before they attack, by arching their backs, raising their heads, and pointing their pectoral fins down.

34. Sharks have a large oil-filled liver that enables them to float.

35. Shark liver oil used to be the main source of vitamin A for humans.

36. The liver of a basking shark can weigh over 1,800 pounds and contain as much as 600 gallons of oil.

37. The Greenland sharks has poisonous flesh that must be boiled three times before eating.

38. The largest fish ever caught with a rod and reel was a Great White shark weighing in at 2,664 pounds and over 16 feet long.

39. The world's most unusual and rarest of sharks is called the Megamouth and wasn't even discovered until 1976. Its mouth can reach up to three feet across, while the rest of the body is about 16 feet long. Only 14 Megamouths have ever been found.

40. The Spiny or Piked Dogfish shark can usually live up to 70 years of age, but some may live until they are 100.

41. Most sharks must constantly swim to force water through their mouths and over their gills to breath. However there are a few shark species that lie flat on the bottom of the ocean.

42. Metal objects gives off weak electric signals in salt water that may confuse sharks causing them to run in to the metal object.

43. The smallest shark is the dwarf lantern shark, which is only seven inches long.

44. Basking sharks are pregnant for more than two years, while other sharks, such as the bonnet head shark, are pregnant for only a few months.

45. Female shark loses her appetite during labor so she won't be tempted to eat her own pups.

46. The 1975 movie *Jaws* fueled so much fear and hatred of sharks, that some species have almost been hunted to extinction.

47. Native Americans in Florida used the teeth of Great White sharks as arrowheads on their arrows.

48. Shark leather can last four times longer than cow hide leather.

49. Angel sharks are so flat that they look like they're part of the sea floor.

50. The Goblin shark is known as the "Frankenshark" because it looks so ugly.

51. Hearing is probably the best of all of a shark's senses. Some sharks can hear prey in the water from a half a mile away.

52. Some sharks can live a year without eating, living off the oil they stored in their bodies.

53. Sharks may use the Earth's magnetic field with special organs that act as a compass to navigate the oceans.

Timeless Classy Insults

These glorious insults are from an era when cleverness with words was still valued; before a great portion of the English language got boiled down to four letter words, not to mention waving middle fingers.

She said, "If you were my husband I'd give you poison,"
and he said, "If you were my wife, I'd drink it."
-Winston Churchill to Lady Astor

"He had delusions of adequacy." - Walter Kerr

"He has all the virtues I dislike and none of the vices I admire." -
-Winston Churchill

"A modest little person, with much to be modest about."
- Winston Churchill

"I have never killed a man, but I have read many obituaries with great pleasure." - Clarence Darrow

"He has never been known to use a word that might send a reader to the dictionary." - William Faulkner (about Ernest Hemingway).
"Poor Faulkner. Does he really think big emotions come from big words?"-Ernest Hemingway (about William Faulkner)

"Thank you for sending me a copy of your book; I'll waste no time reading it." - Moses Hadas

"He can compress the most words into the smallest idea of any man I know." - Abraham Lincoln

"I didn't attend the funeral, but I sent a nice letter saying I approved of it." - Mark Twain

"He has no enemies, but is intensely disliked by his friends." - Oscar Wilde

"I am enclosing two tickets to the first night of my new play; bring a friend....if you have one." - George Bernard Shaw to Winston Churchill

"Cannot possibly attend first night, will attend second... if there is one." - Winston Churchill, in response.

"I feel so miserable without you; it's almost like having you here." -Stephen Bishop

"He is a self-made man and worships his creator." - John Bright

"I've just learned about his illness. Let's hope it's nothing trivial." - Irvin S. Cobb

"He is not only dull himself, he is the cause of dullness in others." 1. Samuel Johnson

"He is simply a shiver looking for a spine to run up." - Paul Keating

"There's nothing wrong with you that reincarnation won't cure."
- Jack E. Leonard

"He has the attention span of a lightning bolt."
- Robert Redford

"They never open their mouths without subtracting from the sum of human knowledge." - Thomas Brackett Reed

"In order to avoid being called a flirt, she always yielded easily."
- Charles, Count Talleyrand

"He loves nature in spite of what it did to him."
- Forrest Tucker

"Why do you sit there looking like an envelope without any address on it?" -
Mark Twain

"His mother should have thrown him away and kept the stork."
- Mae West

"Some cause happiness wherever they go; others, whenever they go."
- Oscar Wilde

"He has Van Gogh's ear for music." - Billy Wilder

"I've had a perfectly wonderful evening But this wasn't it."
- Groucho Marx

How Well Do You Know The Planet You Live On?

1. At one time the earth consisted of one giant land mass and a huge body of water. Geologists today call the land Pangaea.

2. Between 180 and 200 million years ago, Pangaea split into two parts: Laurasia, which consisted of North America, Europe and Asia; and Gondwanaland, which consisted of Africa, South America, India, Antarctica and Australia.

3. Researchers believe that the earth's current stable climate is an anomaly that will end in the next billion years.

4. More than 80% of the Earth's surface is volcanic.

5. The temperature of the earth increases 37 degrees

Fahrenheit per 320 feet after you reach 5 miles below sea level.

6. It is widely believed that earth was originally born as a twin to a planet called Theia. Theia was about half as wide as Earth and roughly the size of Mars. The two planets shared an orbit for several million years until they collided. Earth absorbed Theia, and the remaining debris eventually coagulated into Earth's moon.

7. The theory of Pangaea states that all of Earth's current continents were originally a single supercontinent that existed some 200 million years ago during the Paleozoic and Mesozoic eras.

8. The Earth's plates move just a few inches a year. This means that 250 million years from now, a new supercontinent will be formed.

9. In 1783 an Icelandic eruption threw up enough dust to temporarily block out the sun over Europe.

10. Over 4 million cars in Brazil are now running on gasohol instead of petrol. Gasohol is a fuel made from sugar cane.

11. Without some greenhouse effect, Earth's global temperature would be 0 degrees Fahrenheit (-18 degrees Celsius) rather than 59 degrees F (15 degrees C).

12. The Antarctic ice sheet is 3-4 km thick, covers 13 million sq km and has temperatures as low as -70 degrees centigrade.

13. Earth's Amazon rainforest is home to one third of the planet's land species.

14. There is no land at all at the North Pole, only ice on top of sea.

15. The Arctic Ocean has about 12 million sq km of floating ice and has the coldest winter temperature of -34 degrees centigrade.

16. Earth, which can be viewed as a metal ball coated with rock, hurtles through space at 66,000 miles per hour.

17. The USA uses 29% of the world's petrol and 33% of the

world's electricity.

18. The word "planet" comes from the Greek word *planetai* for "wanderer."

19. Some of the oldest mountains in the world are the Highlands in Scotland. They are estimated to be about 400 million years old.

20. The name "Earth" comes from Old English and Old High Germanic words for "ground" or "soil,".

21. The planet Earth is the only name for a planet of the solar system that does not come from Greco-Roman mythology.

22. The Ancient Egyptians worshipped a sky goddess called Nut.

23. One half to three quarters of Earth's mass is made up of matter that would have made separate planets if not for Earth's cannibalism.

24. Venice in Italy is built on 118 sea islets joined by 400 bridges. It is gradually sinking into the water.

25. Earth is called a terrestrial planet because it is made almost entirely of rock and metal.

26. A huge underground river runs underneath the Nile, with six times more water than the river above.

27. The Earth's moon stabilizes the Earth's tilt. Without the moon, Earth would still have wild changes in climate and probably be uninhabitable.

28. Beaver Lake, in Yellowstone Park, USA, was artificially created by beaver damming.

29. The sun's diameter is over 100 times greater than Earth's, whereas Earth is just about four times larger in diameter than the moon.

30. The desert baobab tree can store up to 1000 liters of water in its trunk.

31. The great impacts that gave Earth its mass could have destroyed the fragile atmosphere that was forming and turn the oceans into steam.

32. An American named Roy Sullivan has been struck by lightning a seven times.

33. Fresh water from the River Amazon can be found up to 180 km out to sea.

34. Earth's ocean of magma was created by meteorites and other space debris crashing into the planet a bit later in its development.

35. The Antarctic Notothenia fish has a protein in its blood that acts like anti-freeze and stops the fish freezing.

36. Earth's unique mix of land and ocean makes the Earth relatively stable by cycling carbon dioxide.

37. Carbon dioxide cycling moderates temperature swings that would otherwise occur.

38. The world's windiest place is Commonwealth Bay, Antarctica.

39. So much energy radiates from inside the Earth that it could satisfy all human energy needs three times over.

40. About 20 to 30 volcanoes erupt each year, mostly under the sea.

41. Although Earth's plates are made of solid rock, they buckle when they collide.

42. The industrial complex of Cubatao in Brazil is known as the Valley of Death because its pollution has destroyed the trees and rivers nearby.

43. The oldest living tree is a California bristlecone pine name 'Methuselah' which is about 4600 years old.

44. Earthquakes, volcanoes, and mountains are all formed by Earth's moving plates.

45. In 1934, a gust of wind reached 371 km/h on Mount Washington in New Hampshire, USA.

46. Other planets and moons in our solar system have volcanoes, but they do not have mountain ranges like Earth's because only Earth has plate tectonics.

47. Lake Bosumtwi in Ghana formed in a hollow made by a meteorite.

48. When a tectonic plate lingers over a hot spot for a while and then moves on, a volcanic island is formed.

49. The White Sea, in Russia, has the lowest temperature, only -2 degrees centigrade. The Persian Gulf is the warmest sea. In the summer its temperature reaches 35.6 degrees centigrade.

50. Off the coast of Florida there is an underwater hotel. Guests have to dive to the entrance.

51. The Himalayas are examples of the movement of tectonic plates against each other.

52. The largest tree in the world is a giant sequoia growing in California. It is 84 meters tall and measures 29 meters round the trunk.

53. The fastest growing tree is the eucalyptus. It can grow 30 feet a year.

Vampire Facts

1. Vampire legends most likely are based on Vlad of Walachia, also known as Vlad the Impaler (c. 1431-1476). He was well known for nailing hats to people's heads, skinning them alive, and impaling them on upright stakes.

2. Vlad the Impaler liked to dip bread into the blood of his enemies and eat it.

3. Vlad, means son of the dragon or Dracula, who has been identified as the historical Dracula.

4. Vlad the Impaler was murdered in 1476, his tomb is reported empty.

5. A group a vampires has been called a clutch, brood, coven, pack, or a clan.

6. The most famous vampire of all time, Count Dracula, quoted Deuteronomy 12:23: "The blood is the life."

7. Supposedly you can deter a vampire by throwing seeds (usually mustard) outside a door.

8. Another way to supposedly deter a vampire is to place fishing net outside a window.

9. Vampires are compelled to count the seeds or the holes in the net, delaying them until the sun comes up.

10. Prehistoric stone monuments called "dolmens" have been found over the graves of the dead in northwest Europe to keep vampires from rising.

11. A rare disease called *porphyria* (also called the "vampire" or "Dracula" disease) causes vampire-like symptoms, such as an extreme sensitivity to sunlight and sometimes hairiness. In some cases, teeth become stained reddish brown, and eventually the patient may go mad.

12. Haematodipsia, is a sexual thirst for blood.

13. Anemia ("bloodlessness") was often mistaken for a symptom of a vampire attack.

14. Countess Elizabeth Bathory (1560-1614) was accused of biting the flesh of girls while torturing them and bathing in their blood to retain her youthful beauty. She was by all accounts a very attractive woman but a known as a vampire.

15. The earliest account of vampires is found in an ancient Sumerian and Babylonian myth dating to 4,000 B.C. The myth describes a *ekimmu* or *edimmu* (one who is snatched away). The *ekimmu* is a type of *uruku* or *utukku* which translates to a spirit or demon who was not buried properly and has returned as a vengeful spirit to suck the life out of the living.

16. The book *Pert em Hru* (Egyptian Book of the Dead), states that if the *ka* (one of the five parts of the soul) does not receive particular offerings, it ventures out of its tomb as a *kha* to find nourishment, which may include drinking the blood of the living.

17. The Egyptian goddess Sekhmet was known to drink blood.

18. The ancient fanged goddess Kali of India also had a powerful desire for blood.

19. Chinese vampires were called a *ch'iang shih* (corpse-hopper) and had red eyes and crooked claws. They were said to have a strong sexual drive that led them to attack women. As they grew stronger, the *ch'iang shih* gained the ability to fly, grew long white hair, and could also change into a wolf.

20. While both vampires and zombies generally belong to the "undead," there are differences between them depending on the mythology from which they emerged. For example, zombies tend to have a lower IQ than vampires, prefer brains and flesh rather than strictly blood, are immune to garlic, most likely have a reflection in the mirror, are based largely in African myth, move more slowly due to rotting muscles, can enter churches, and are not necessarily afraid of fire or sunlight.

21. Vampire hysteria and corpse mutilations to "kill" suspected vampires were so pervasive in Europe during the mid-eighteenth century that some rulers created laws to prevent

the unearthing of bodies. In some areas, mass hysteria led to public executions of people believed to be vampires.

22. The first full work of fiction about a vampire in English was John Polidori's influential *The Vampyre*, which was published incorrectly under Lord Byron's name. Polidori (1795-1821) was Byron's doctor and based his vampire on Byron.

23. The first vampire movie is supposedly *Secrets of House No. 5* in 1912. F.W. Murnau's silent black-and-white *Nosferatu* came soon after, in 1922. However, it was Tod Browning's *Dracula*—with the erotic, charming, cape- and tuxedo-clad aristocrat played by Bela Lugosi—that became the hallmark of vampire movies and literature.

24. A vampire supposedly has control over the animal world and can turn into a bat, rat, owl, moth, fox, or wolf.

25. In 2009, a sixteenth-century female skull with a rock wedged in its mouth was found near the remains of plague victims. It was not unusual during that century to shove a rock or brick in the mouth of a suspected vampire to prevent it from feeding on the bodies of other plague victims or attacking the living. Female vampires were also often blamed for spreading the bubonic plague throughout Europe.

26. Joseph Sheridan Le Fany's gothic 1872 novella about a female vampire, "Carmilla," is considered the prototype for female and lesbian vampires and greatly influenced Bram Stoker's own *Dracula*. In the story, Carmilla is eventually discovered as a vampire and, true to folklore remedies, she is staked in her blood-filled coffin, beheaded, and cremated.

27. Bram Stoker's *Dracula* (1897) remains an enduring influence on vampire mythology and has never gone out of print. Some scholars say it is clearly a Christian allegory; others suggest it contains covert psycho-sexual anxieties reflective of the Victorian era.

28. According to several legends, if someone was bitten by a suspected vampire, he or she should drink the ashes of a burned vampire. To prevent an attack, a person should make bread with the blood of vampire and eat it.

29. Thresholds have historically held significant symbolic value, and a vampire cannot cross a threshold unless invited. The connection between threshold and vampires seems to be a concept of complicity or allowance. Once a commitment is made to allow evil, evil can re-enter at any time.

30. Before Christianity, methods of repelling vampires included garlic, hawthorn branches, rowan trees (later used to make crosses), scattering of seeds, fire, decapitation with a gravedigger's spade, salt (associated with preservation and purity), iron, bells, a rooster's crow, peppermint, running water, and burying a suspected vampire at a crossroads. It was also not unusual for a corpse to be buried face down so it would dig down the wrong way and become lost in the earth.

31. After the advent of Christianity, methods of repelling vampires began to include holy water, crucifixes, and Eucharist wafers. These methods were usually not fatal to the vampire, and their effectiveness depended on the belief of the user.

32. Garlic, a traditional vampire repellent, has been used as a form of protection for over 2,000 years. The ancient Egyptians believed garlic was a gift from God, Roman soldiers thought it gave them courage, sailors believed it protected them from shipwreck, and German miners believed it protected them from evil spirits when they went underground. In several cultures, brides carried garlic under their clothes for protection, and cloves of garlic were used to protect people from a wide range of illnesses. Modern-day scientists found that the oil in garlic, allicin, is a highly effective antibiotic.

33. That sunlight can kill vampires seems to be a modern invention, perhaps started by the U.S. government to scare superstitious guerrillas in the Philippines in the 1950s. While sunlight can be used by vampires to kill other vampires, as in Ann Rice's popular novel *Interview with a Vampire*, other vampires such as Lord Ruthven and Varney were able to walk in daylight.

34. The legend that vampires must sleep in coffins probably arose from reports of gravediggers and morticians who described corpses suddenly sitting up in their graves or coffins. This eerie phenomenon could be caused by the decomposing process.

35. According to some legends, a vampire may engage in sex with his former wife, which often led to pregnancy. In fact, this belief may have provided a convenient explanation as to why a widow, who was supposed to be celibate, became pregnant. The resulting child was called a *gloglave* (pl. *glog*) in Bulgarian or *vampirdzii* in Turkish. Rather than being ostracized, the child was considered a hero who had powers to slay a vampire.

36. The Twilight book series (*Twilight*, *New Moon*, *Eclipse*, and *Breaking Dawn*) by Stephanie Meyers has also become popular with movie-goers. Meyers admits that she did not research vampire mythology. Indeed, her vampires break tradition in several ways. For example, garlic, holy items, and sunlight do not harm them. Some critics praise the book for capturing teenage feelings of sexual tension and alienation.

37. Hollywood and literary vampires typically deviate from folklore vampires. For example, Hollywood vampires are typically pale, aristocratic, very old, need their native soil, are supernaturally beautiful, and usually need to be bitten to become a vampire. In contrast, folklore vampires (before Bram Stoker) are usually peasants, recently dead, initially appear as shapeless "bags of blood," do not need their native soil, and are often cremated with or without being staked.

38. Folklore vampires can become vampires not only through a bite, but also if they were once a werewolf, practiced sorcery, were excommunicated, committed suicide, were an illegitimate child of parents who were illegitimate, or were still born or died before baptism. In addition, anyone who has eaten the flesh of a sheep killed by a wolf, was a seventh son, was the child of a pregnant woman who was looked upon by a vampire, was a nun who stepped over an

unburied body, had teeth when they were born, or had a cat jump on their corpse before being buried could also turn into vampires.

39. In vampire folklore, a vampire initially emerges as a soft blurry shape with no bones. He was "bags of blood" with red, glowing eyes and, instead of a nose, had a sharp snout that he sucked blood with. If he could survive for 40 days, he would then develop bones and a body and become much more dangerous and difficult to kill.

40. While blood drinking isn't enough to define a vampire, it is an overwhelming feature. In some cultures, drinking the blood of a victim allowed the drinker to absorb their victim's strength, take on an animal's quality, or even make a woman more fecund. The color red is also involved in many vampire rituals.

41. In some vampire folktales, vampires can marry and move to another city where they take up jobs suitable for vampires, such as butchers, barbers, and tailors. That they become butchers may be based on the analogy that butchers are descendants of the "sacrificer."

42. Certain regions in the Balkans believed that fruit, such as pumpkins or watermelons, would become vampires if they were left out longer than 10 days or not consumed by Christmas. Vampire pumpkins or watermelons generally were not feared because they do not have teeth. A drop of blood on a fruit's skin is a sign that it is about to turn into a vampire.

43. Mermaids can also be vampires—but instead of sucking blood, they suck out the breath of their victims.

44. By the end of the twentieth century, over 300 motion pictures were made about vampires, and over 100 of them featured Dracula. Over 1,000 vampire novels were published, most within the past 25 years.

45. The most popular vampire in children's fiction in recent years had been *Bunnicula*, the cute little rabbit that lives a happy existence as a vegetarian vampire.

46. Some historians argue that Prince Charles is a direct descendant of the Vlad the Impaler, the son of Vlad Dracula.

47. The best known recent development of vampire mythology is *Buffy the Vampire Slayer* and its spin-off, *Angel.* Buffy is interesting because it contemporizes vampirism in the very real, twentieth-century world of a teenager vampire slayer played by Sarah Michelle Gellar and her "Scooby gang." It is also notable because the show has led to the creation of "Buffy Studies" in academia.

Truly Unique Household Tips

Here are some truly unique and not so widely known tips and tricks to use around the house.

Reheating Pizza

Heat up leftover pizza in a nonstick skillet on top of the stove. Set heat to med-low and heat till warm. This keeps the crust crispy. No soggy micro pizza. I saw this on the cooking channel and it really works.

Make Easy Deviled Eggs

Put cooked egg yolks in a zip lock bag. Seal, mash till they are all broken up. Add remainder of ingredients, reseal, keep mashing it up mixing thoroughly. Cut the tip of the baggy, squeeze mixture into egg. Just throw bag away when done easy clean up.

Expanding Frosting

When you buy a container of cake frosting from the store, whip it with your mixer for a few minutes. You can double it in size. You get to frost more cake or cupcakes with the same amount. You also eat less sugar and calories per serving.

Reheating Refrigerated Bread

To warm biscuits, pancakes, or muffins that were refrigerated, place Them in a microwave with a cup of water. The increased moisture will Keep the food moist and help it reheat faster.

Use Newspaper to Make Weeds Go Away

Start putting in your plants; work the nutrients in your soil. Wet newspapers put layers around the plants overlapping as you go cover with mulch and forget about weeds. Weeds will get through some gardening plastic they will not get through wet newspapers.

Cleaning Broken Glass

Use a dry cotton ball to pick up little broken pieces of glass
The fibers catch ones you can't see!

No More Mosquitoes

Place a dryer sheet in your pocket. It will keep the mosquitoes away.
Keep Squirrels Away From Your Plants
To keep squirrels from eating your plants sprinkle your plants with
cayenne pepper. The cayenne pepper doesn't hurt the plant and the
squirrels won't come near it.

Reducing Static Cling

Pin a small safety pin to the seam of your slip and you will not
have a clingy skirt or dress. Same thing works with slacks that cling
when wearing panty hose. Place pin in seam of slacks and - voila –
static is gone.

No Stick Measuring Cups

Before you pour sticky substances into a measuring cup, fill it with
hot water. Dump out the hot water, but don't dry the cup. Next, add
Your ingredient, such as peanut butter, and watch how easily it comes
right out.

No More Foggy Windshield

Hate foggy windshields? Buy a chalkboard eraser and keep it in the
glove box of your car. When the windows fog, rub with the eraser!

Hair Conditioner to Shave?

Use your hair conditioner to shave your legs. It's a lot cheaper
Than shaving cream and leaves your legs really smooth. It's also great
way to use up the conditioner you bought but didn't like when you
tried it in your hair.

Say Goodbye Fruit Flies

To get rid of pesky fruit flies, take a small glass fill it 1/2" with apple Cider Vinegar and 2 drops of dishwashing liquid, mix well. You will find those flies drawn to the cup and gone forever!

Get Rid of Ants

Put small piles of cornmeal where you see ants. They eat it, take it "home," & can't digest it so it kills them. It may take a week or so, And it is safe for pets or small children.

Men Are From Where?

1. Mars was formed about 4.5 billion years ago and is about 4,000 miles wide (half the diameter of Earth).

2. Much of Earth is covered by oceans, because of that the amount of land surface of the two planets is nearly equal.

3. Mars is also much lighter than Earth, with only 1/10 of its mass.

4. Mars is the fourth planet from the sun and is the last terrestrial rocky planet . The outer planets are all gaseous.

5. Driving 60 mph in a car, it would take 271 years and 221 days to get to Mars from Earth.

6. The average temperature on Mars is $-81°$ and can range from $-205°$ in the winter to $72°$ Fahrenheit in the summer.

7. Mars lacks an ozone layer; therefore, the surface of Mars is bathed in a lethal dose of radiation every time the sun rises.

8. During a Mars winter, almost 20% of the air freezes.

9. The Egyptians gave Mars its first recorded name: *Har dècher* ("The red one"). The Babylonians called it *Nergal* ("Star of death"). The Greeks and Romans named the planet after their respective gods of war, Ares and Mars. The Hebrews called it *Ma'adim*, or "One who blushes." Many ancient people believed the reddish color came from actual blood on the planet.

10. Mars' crust is thicker than Earth's and is made up of one piece, unlike Earth's crust which consists of several moving plates.

11. The month of March is named after Mars.

12. The symbol for Mars looks like a shield and a spear from the war god Mars/Ares. It is also the symbol for the male sex.

13. The ancient Greeks thought that Earth was the center of the universe and that Mars was one of the five traveling

stars that revolved around it.

14. Egyptians called Mars the "the backward traveler" because Mars appeared to move backwards through the zodiac every 25.7 months.

15. Mars' red color is due to iron oxide, also known as rust, and has the consistency of talcum powder. Literally, the metallic rocks on Mars are rusting.

16. The atmosphere (mostly made up of carbon dioxide) on Mars is so thin that water cannot exist in liquid form—it can exist only as water vapor or ice. Liquid water is considered for many scientists to be the "holy grail" of Mars.

17. No human could survive the low pressure of Mars. If you went to Mars without an appropriate space suit, the oxygen in your blood would literally turn into bubbles, causing immediate death.

18. Mars contains the largest labyrinth of intersecting canyons in the solar system called the Noctis Labyrinthus ("labyrinth of the night").

19. Mars has the largest and most violent dust storms in our entire solar system. These storms often have winds topping 125 mph, can last for weeks, and can cover the entire planet. They usually occur when Mars is closest to the sun.

20. Only 1/3 of spacecrafts sent to Mars have been successful, leading some scientists to wonder if there is a Martian "Bermuda triangle" or a "Great Galactic Ghoul" that likes to eat spacecraft.

21. In 1976, Viking I photographed a mesa on Mars that had the appearance of a human face. Many individuals and organizations interested in extraterrestrial life argued that intelligent beings created the "Face."

22. Mars has an enormous canyon named Valles Marineris (Mariner Valley) which is an astounding 2,500 miles long and four miles deep. As long as the continental United States, this gigantic canyon was likely formed by the tectonic "cracking" of Mars' crust and is the longest known crevice

in the solar system.

23. During the Renaissance, Mars played a central role in one of the most important and fiercest intellectual battles in the history of Western civilization: whether Earth is the center of the universe. Nicholas Copernicus (1473-1543) coherently explained that Mars seems to move backwards across the sky because Earth overtakes Mars in its orbit around the sun.

24. The Earth environment most closely resembling the current conditions of Mars is that of the Antarctic deserts.

25. The most hostile environments on Earth are far more suitable for life than the surface of Mars.

26. Although it is much colder on Mars than on Earth, the similar tilt of Earth's and Mars' axes means they have similar seasons. Like Earth's, Mars' north and south polar caps shrink in the summer and grow in the winter. In addition, a day on Mars is 24 hours 37 minutes—nearly the same as Earth's. No other planet shares such similar characteristics with Earth.

27. Mars' seasons are twice as long as those on Earth because it takes Mars 687 days to orbit the sun, twice as long as Earth's 365-day journey.

28. With no large moon like Earth's to stabilize it, Mars periodically tilts much more toward the sun, creating warmer summers on Mars than it otherwise would have.

29. Mars is home to Hellas, a vast and featureless plain that covers 1300 miles (the size of the Caribbean Sea). It was created by asteroids crashing into the planet's surface of Mars nearly four billion years ago.

30. Mars' moon Phobos ("fear") rises in the west and sets in the east—twice a day. Deimos ("panic"), on the other hand, takes 2.7 days to rise in the east and set in the west. The moons are named after the twin gods who accompanied Ares (or Mars) into battle.

31. Mars' moon Phobos (fear) rises in the west and sets in the east—twice a day. Deimos (panic), on the other hand, takes

2.7 days to rise in the east and set in the west. Mars' moons are so named because the twin gods—panic and fear—accompanied Ares (or Mars) into battle.

32. Phobos orbits remarkably close to Mars and is gradually sinking into the Red Planet. In about 50 million years it will either crash into Mars or break up and form a small ring around the planet.

33. Mars has no magnetic field, indicating that it does not have a molten metal core, like Earth does. However, there is evidence that Mars once had a magnetic field and that the field experienced reversals, much like Earth's magnetic field which reverses every few thousand years.

34. Mars has 37.5% of the gravity that Earth has. This means that a 100-pound person on Earth would weigh only 38 pounds on Mars and could jump three times as high.

35. Mars is home to the highest peak in the solar system: Olympus Mons. This towering peak is 15 miles high (three times higher than Mt. Everest) and has a diameter of 375 miles (the size of Arizona). It is called a shield volcano because it has such a wide base and rises very gradually.

36. Most researchers believe that Mars' surface was shaped by catastrophic floods billions of years ago.

37. Scientists are unclear on what form water may have taken early in Mars' history. One theory is that early Mars was warmer and boasted rain and oceans. Another theory is that Mars was always very cold, but water trapped underground as ice was periodically released when heating caused the ice to melt and gush to the surface.

38. No one knows what happened to the water on Mars. Many scientists speculate that Mars' water may have been lost into space if the atmosphere of Mars thinned out over many eons. Large quantities of water, in either ice or liquid form, are thought to be still trapped underneath its surface.

39. In 1965, the United States spacecraft Mariner 4 made the first successful flyby of Mars. It took 228 days to reach Mars and sent 22 images to Earth. Many scientists were extremely

disappointed that the images showed no signs of oceans or vegetation that they thought it would find. In 2008, however, scientists believe they found significant evidence of carbonates in certain regions on Mars, which suggests that liquid water and perhaps even life once existed there.

40. On November 14, 1971, the United States' Mariner 9 was the first spacecraft to orbit Mars (or any other planet). After a massive dust storm cleared, Mariner 9 began transmitting nearly 73,000 images and revealing enormous volcanoes, huge canyons, frozen underground water in the form of permafrost, and what appeared to be dried-up river beds.

41. Mars 2, built by the former Soviet Union, has the bittersweet distinction of being the first human-built object to touch down on Mars in November 1971. Unfortunately, it crashed into the surface during a massive dust storm.

42. July 20, 1976, was historic because the United States' Viking 1 was the first human spacecraft to land intact and operational on the surface of Mars. Viking 2 followed, landing successfully on September 3, 1976. The Viking Landers relayed the first color pictures of the planet. When the second Viking had its last moments of contact in 1978, project manager George Gianopoulos said "It's like losing an old friend; how do you express it?"

43. During the Viking missions to Mars, scientists were worried about contaminating the Martian environment with microbes from Earth.

44. In 1996, the United States launched Pathfinder (also called the Sagan Lander after famed astronomer and author Carl Sagan) so that it would land on America's Independence Day July 4, 1997. It bounced for 92 seconds on airbags before stopping, making it the first successful air bag-mediated touchdown.

45. Pathfinder's small robot, Sojourner, collected and studied Martian rocks. It moved less than .5 inches per second so that if it ran into trouble, scientists wearing 3-D glasses to gauge depth and perspective on their 2-D computers on Earth could send it precise directions. Sojourner was the

first robot to explore another planet.

46. The unofficial names of many rocks on the surface of Mars are easy-going names, such as Barnacle Bill, Yogi, Pop-Tart, Shark, Half Dome, Moe, Stimpy, and Cabbage Patch. Scientists chose these names because they were convenient to remember.

47. Only 12 Martian meteors are known to exist on earth and are collectively called Shergotty-Nakhla-Chassingy or SNC ("snick") meteorites. The most famous one is called Allan Hills (ALH) 84001 and is believed to have blasted off Mars 16 million years ago, hitting Earth 13,000 years ago in Antarctica. It is so remarkable because it appears to hold microscopic fossils of Martian bacteria, sparking intense debate about whether ancient life ever existed on Mars.

48. Until recently, it was thought that Mars' polar caps were made from carbon dioxide (dry ice) with only a small amount of water. Later observations indicated that the polar caps were mostly frozen water with a thin layer of carbon dioxide.

49. If melted into liquid form, the amount of water in the southern polar cap would cover the entire planet to a depth of about 36 feet.

50. Galileo Galilee was the first person to observe Mars through a telescope, in 1609.

51. On August 27, 2003, Mars made its closest approach to Earth in nearly 60,000 years. The next time it will be that close again will be in 2287.

52. In 1877, Italian astronomer Giovanni Schiaparelli discovered a strange network of lines on Mars and called them *canali*, Italian for "channels" but which was mistranslated as "canals." American astronomer Percival Lowell (wrongly) guessed that the canals were used to move water from the Martian ice caps to the desert. His work sparked great public fascination with Mars.

53. H.G. Wells' 1898 novel *The War of the Worlds* portrays Martians as technologically advanced invaders who destroy

thousands of lives in their attempt to take over the world. Its 1938 public radio broadcast by actor Orson Wells incited mass panic across the United States.

54. Mars' northern and southern hemispheres are so different they could be different planets. The southern hemisphere is heavily cratered with a high elevation. In contrast, the northern hemisphere has a lower elevation with fewer craters. Scientists believe a meteor the size of Pluto once hit Mars, creating the smoother northern region of the planet.

Volcanoes Can Be Fun? I Think...

1. "*Volcano*" is from the Latin *Volcanus* or Vulcan, the Roman god of fire.

2. "*Lava*" derives from the Latin *lavara*, meaning "to wash," and is magma that has erupted at the surface. Lava can flow up to speeds of 62 miles per hour.

3. "*Magma*" is Latin for "dregs of ointment," which derives from the Proto Indo-European *mag* meaning "kneading." The term "magma" in its geological sense as molten rock was first used in 1865.[c]

4. When the top of a volcano top collapses, it forms a caldera, which is Spanish for "kettle."

5. The ancient Greeks thought that the god of Fire, Hephaestus, lived beneath Mt. Etna.

6. The Titan god Prometheus is said to have stolen fire from Hephaestus's volcano to give to humans.

7. Hundreds of years ago, the Aztecs of Mexico and the people of Nicaragua believed gods lived in lava lakes. They would sacrifice beautiful young girls to these powerful gods.

8. Well into the middle Ages, many believed volcanoes were entrances into the fiery underworld.

9. The worst volcanic disaster of the twentieth century is considered to be the eruption of Mt. Pelée in 1902. It happened on the island of Martinique in the Caribbean and killed 30,121 people. Two people survived: a shoemaker living on the edge of the island and a prisoner who had been locked in a dungeon cell with thick stone walls.

10. The loudest noise ever known was produced by a volcanic eruption at Krakatoa, near Javan, in 1883. The sound was heard in Australia, 5000 km away.

11. When Laki volcano in Iceland erupted in 1783, its lava flow stretched 65 km, the longest ever recorded.

12. About 20 per cent of all volcanoes are underwater.

13. About 20 to 30 volcanoes erupt each year, mostly under the sea.

14. Lava from an erupting volcano may be as hot as 1200 degrees centigrade.

15. During the past 400 years, nearly a quarter of a million people have been killed as a direct result of volcanic eruptions.

16. Indirect aftereffects such as famine, climate changes, and disease most likely have tripled that number.

17. A species of bird called a maleo uses heat given out by warm volcanic sand to incubate its large eggs. When the chicks hatch, they burrow their way to the surface of the sand.

18. Today's most active and dangerous volcano today is Popocatépetl, nicknamed El Popo, which is just 33 miles from Mexico City. El Popo is still active, sending thousands of tons of gas and ash into the air each year.

19. Did you know there are no active volcanoes in Australia? The continent sits in the middle of a tectonic plate.

20. Volcanic areas have some of the most fertile farmland in the world. Volcanic eruptions bring nutrients such as potassium and phosphorus to the Earth's soil. The weathering of volcanic rocks also releases nutrients.

21. The material ejected from a volcano is called "pyroclastic flow" from the Greek *pyro* (fire) and *I* (broken). It includes small fragments of rock, frothy pumice, and large boulders. Pyroclastic flow can reach temperatures of 212° F and can rocket down the side of a mountain at 155 m.p.h.

22. In 1963, an undersea volcano created the newest land mass on Earth, Surtsey Island, which lies off the southwest coast of Iceland. Today Surtsey is about 1 sq. mile and is named after Surt, a fire giant from Norse mythology.

23. There are approximately 1,500 active volcanoes, not counting undersea volcanoes. Of these, only about 20-30 erupt in any one year.

24. Volcanologists measure the size of an eruption with the Volcanic Explosivity Index (VEI), with 0 being the weakest and 8 the strongest. Eight is usually reserved for super eruptions, popularly called "super volcanoes."

25. Iceland is made up almost entirely of volcanic rocks like those found on the ocean floor. It gradually built up above sea level through intense and prolonged eruptions.

26. In 2010, a large volcano in Iceland shut down air traffic for much of the European Union.

27. The Lake Toba super volcanic eruption nearly 75,000 years ago in Indonesia plunged earth into a volcanic winter now known as the Millennium Ice Age. It is believed to be responsible for the formation of sulfuric acid in the atmosphere.

28. Mount St. Helens in Washington erupted on May 18, 1980. The eruption had 500 times the power of an atomic bomb. Geologists considered this a moderate eruption. 37 people who didn't heed warnings died in the eruption.

29. The Pacific Ring of Fire is the boundary of the large Pacific plate which is slowly sub ducting under or grinding past other plates. Most of the world's biggest volcanoes are concentrated here

30. In A.D. 79, Vesuvius erupted violently, devastating the towns of Pompeii and Herculaneum. Eyewitness accounts of the time, recent excavations, and the preserved remains tell the horrific story of the eruption.

31. In 1660, the people of Naples were shocked to find what looked like little black crosses raining down on them. While they thought it was proof that St. Januarius was looking out for them, the crosses were really twin pyroxene crystals which Mt. Vesuvius spewed out of its crater. Vesuvius last erupted in 1944.

32. New ocean floor is created when two oceanic plates move apart and magma bubbles up to fill the rift. This is called a rift volcano. Through this process, the Atlantic Ocean is widening by 2 cm. per year, and the East Pacific Rise is widening by 20 cm. a year. In 10 million years, the East Pacific Rise will be 1,240 miles wider.

33. Pele is the Hawaiian goddess of fire and volcanoes and was thought to live in the crater of the Kilauea volcano on Hawaii. She is said to have a terrible temper and will throw lava at anyone who angers her. Some people have been known to send back lava samples they have taken from the Hawaiian Volcanoes National Park because of the bad luck they associate with Pele.

34. The three main types of volcano shapes are shield, cinder cone, and stratovolcano. Stratovolcanoes, also called composite volcanoes, are the most common type of volcanoes and often have symmetrical steep slopes. Classic examples include Mount Rainer in Washington State and Mount Fuji in Japan.

35. The largest caldera is the La Garita Caldera in Colorado which was formed 26-28 million years ago.

36. Some volcanic islands such as Iceland and Hawaii have black beaches. Their sand is made from basalt, an igneous

rock formed when lava cools and has been broken down into sand particles.

37. Tambora's 1815 massive eruption and its devastating effects are said to have inspired Lord Byron's gloomy poem "Darkness" (1816) and Mary Shelley's immortal novel *Frankenstein* (1818).

38. Yellowstone National Park in Wyoming sits on the site of an ancient super volcano. It erupted around 2 million years ago, 1.3 million years ago, and 640,000 years ago. If it follows the same pattern, another eruption is due any time now. Scary.

39. Japan has over 10% of the world's active volcanoes.

40. More than 300 million people (nearly 1 in 20) live in the shadow of active volcanoes, including Mount Vesuvius in Italy, Mount Rainer in the U.S., and Popocatepetl in Mexico.

41. In some volcanic areas such as Iceland, heat energy from magma can be used to warm water and run power plants. This type of energy is called geothermal (earth heat) energy.

42. When Paricutin in Mexico erupted from 1943-1952, no one was killed by ash, rocks, lava, gases, or mud flows, though three people died from being struck by volcanic lightening.

43. In 1943, a Mexican farmer named Dionisio Pulido witnessed the birth of a volcano in his cornfield about 329 kilometers west of Mexico City. It started as a slight depression in his field and soon became a fissure that emitted smoke and hissing noises. During the next nine years, the volcano Paricutin had grown to an elevation of 2,272 meters and its voluminous lava flows had destroyed several towns.

44. The 1815, volcano Tambora in Indonesia was the greatest volcanic eruption observed by humans and killed over 70,000 people. Effects were felt as far as Europe and North America, including prolonged inclement weather which resulted in food riots and the worst famine in the nineteenth century.

45. In August 1986, a cloud mixture of carbon dioxide and water rose from Lake Nyos, a crater lake in Cameroon (western Africa). The heavy gas cloud flowed downhill and gathered in the valleys, asphyxiating 1,700 people and 3,500 livestock living in the villages below.

46. An acid lake in the crater of Kawah-Idjen in Indonesia absorbs gases rising from the volcano, creating a lake so toxic it can burn through human flesh in minutes.

47. The earliest known picture of a volcano is the nearly 8,000-year-old wall painting of an eruption of Hasan Dag volcano in Turkey. The houses of a town, Çatalhöyük, can be seen at the mountain's base.

48. In Japan, "baths" in warm volcanic sand are believed to cure many illnesses.

49. The largest volcano found in the solar system is Olympus Mons on Mars, though it is now extinct.

50. Venus may have at one time produced more volcanoes than any other planet in our solar system, though they are all now extinct.

51. While no other planet besides Earth shows active volcanoes, Io, one of Jupiter's moons, shows volcanoes that are erupting.

52. The 1883 eruption of Krakatau in Indonesia is thought to have released 200 megatons of energy, the equivalent of 15,000 nuclear bombs. Even though the island was uninhabited, the eruption killed 36,000 people as the result of burning ash showers and huge tsunamis. It generated the loudest sound historically reported.

53. The most lava ever recorded from a single eruption was the 1783 Laki eruption in Iceland. Though there was no single big explosion, this eruption killed one fourth of Iceland's population by producing poisonous gases and clouds of ash that resulted in widespread crop failure and starvation.

54. In January 2009, scientists from the Alaska volcano observatory warned that Mt. Redoubt, a peak just 100 miles southwest of Anchorage, could erupt anytime. Mt Redoubt

last erupted in 1989, shooting ash high into the jet stream, causing engine failure in a KLM jet carrying 231 passengers. The plane dropped more than 2 miles before the crew could restart the engines.

Which Came First? The Chicken or the Egg?

This is one of the oldest questions which was even tackled by Einstein and left unanswered. This question has perplexed almost every generations. But now the question, "Which came first, the chicken or the egg?" has been solved!

In a 2010 study called "Structural Control of Crystal Nuclei by an Eggshell Protein", British scientists claim to have finally come up with the definitive answer to the chicken and the egg question.

The scientific researchers at Sheffield and Warwick universities have found that a protein found only in a chicken's ovaries is necessary for the formation of the egg. The egg can therefore only exist if it has been created inside a female chicken also known as a "hen".

The researchers say that the protein speeds up the development of the hard shell, which is essential in protecting the delicate yolk and fluids while the chick grows inside the egg, according to the report.

Many years ago the same protein had been identified long before it was linked to egg formation.

Question answered. It was the Chicken.

The Earth Is Small. The Sun is Big

1. A lightning bolt can generate heat, five times hotter than the surface of the sun.

2. The sun is orbited by eight major planets: Mercury, Venus, Earth, Mars, Jupiter, Saturn, Uranus, and Neptune. Go back to school and you will learn Pluto is no longer classified as a planet.

3. Our sun is classified as a "G2 dwarf" size star due to its size, heat, and chemical makeup. For a star it is only about medium sized.

4. The sun is about 149.60 million kilometers or 92.96 million miles away from earth.

5. The sun is about 330,330 times bigger than our puny little planet earth. It would take approximately 109 planet Earths to cover the surface of the sun and more than one million planet Earths would fit inside of the sun.

6. About four million tons of hydrogen are consumed by the sun every second. It would take 100 trillion tons of dynamite to be detonated every second to match the energy produced by the sun.

7. Scientists have determined that the sun will continue to burn hydrogen for another four or five billion years or so, before it switches to helium as a primary fuel. Don't expect it to get cooler though, after that it gets bigger and hotter.

8. Every 11 years or so, the sun's solar activity surges. Sunspots appear on the surface of the sun. These sunspots can explode hurtling massive clouds of gas known as "CMEs" through the solar system.

9. Don't rely on your compass if you ever visit the sun. Every 11 years or so the sun reverses its overall magnetic polarity. The north magnetic pole becomes a south pole, and vice versa.

10. At its core, the sun's temperature is about 15 million degrees Celsius (about 27 million degrees Fahrenheit).

11. An earth's day is a complete rotation of the earth which takes approximately 24 hours. The sun rotates on its axis once every for 25.38 Earth days. Making each day on the sun about 609 hours.

12. If the sun were a cooler place to visit you would probably want to work out a lot before you go. If you are an average person weighing 150 pounds on Earth, you would weigh 4,200 pounds on the sun because the sun's gravity is about 28 times that of the Earth.

13. In ancient Egypt, the sun god Ra was the dominant figure among the high gods. He achieved the highest status because he was believed to have created himself and the eight other gods they worshipped.

14. The small measured changes in the sun's radiation output from one decade to the next are only about one-tenth of 1 percent, not even large enough to really provide a detectable signal in Earth's surface temperature record. Al Gore likes to blame us humans for the increase in global temperatures. Maybe we should send him more money for a carbon offset so he can fix it. That would be another debate.

15. During about a 75-year period beginning in 1645, astronomers detected almost no sunspot activity on the sun. They called this period the "Maunder Minimum". This event coincided with the coldest part of the Little Ice Age which was a 350-year cold spell that gripped much of Europe and North America. Scientific estimates now determine that the change in brightness was perhaps not enough to create this global cooling. Based on current estimates, even if another Maunder Minimum were to occur to us in this day and age. It might result in an average temperature decrease of about 2 degrees Fahrenheit.

A Childs Poem Brings Life Down To Earth

In late 2010 a poem was sent through chain e-mail. It was in mass distribution but puts our current state of the country in to perspective. Here is the poem:

Now I sit me down in school
Where praying is against the rule
For this great nation under God
Finds mention of Him very odd.

If scripture now the class recites,
It violates the Bill of Rights.
And anytime my head I bow
Becomes a Federal matter now.

Our hair can be purple, orange or green,
That's no offense; it's a freedom scene..
The law is specific, the law is precise.
Prayers spoken aloud are a serious vice.

For praying in a public hall
Might offend someone with no faith at all..
In silence alone we must meditate,
God's name is prohibited by the state.

We're allowed to cuss and dress like freaks,
And pierce our noses, tongues and cheeks...
They've outlawed guns, but FIRST the Bible.
To quote the Good Book makes me liable.

We can elect a pregnant Senior Queen,
And the 'unwed daddy,' our Senior King.
It's 'inappropriate' to teach right from wrong,
We're taught that such 'judgments' do not belong..

We can get our condoms and birth controls,
Study witchcraft, vampires and totem poles.
But the Ten Commandments are not allowed,
No word of God must reach this crowd.

It's scary here I must confess,
When chaos reigns the school's a mess.
So, Lord, this silent plea I make:
Should I be shot; My soul please take!
Amen

--Author Unknown

For Your Health

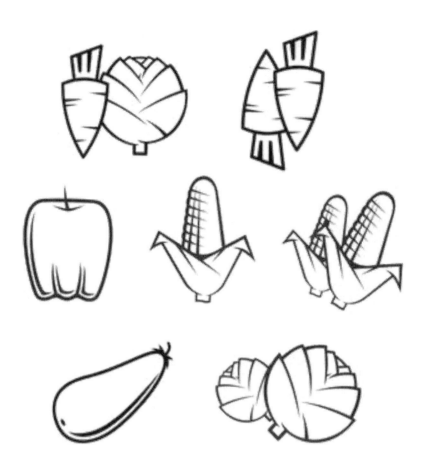

How bad is junk food really?

1. Junk food is often defined as foods with little nutritional value and high in calories, sugar, fat, caffeine, and/or salt. Junk food can include anything from everyday breakfast cereals to chips, soda, candy, French fries, even gum, hot dogs, and hamburgers.

2. The term "junk food" started in the 1960s but became more popular after the hit song "junk food junkie" hit the top in 1976.

3. The increase in people with obesity, high blood pressure, heart disease and other diseases and cancers is often linked to the increase of junk food production in the past decade

4. In the case the "Twinkie Defense" In 1979 a man named Daniel White stated he killed San Francisco mayor George Moscone and Harvey milk due to the massive amount of junk food such as Twinkies, cupcakes and candy he consumed, which caused a chemical imbalance in his brain. He was still convicted and, in 1981, Congress outlawed the "Twinkie Defense."

5. Fats in junk food trigger chemicals in the brain to want more of that food. This effect can last for several days.

6. Over $2 billion worth of candy is sold every Halloween, more than any other holiday.

7. On Saturday morning children shows Almost 80% of food commercials aired are for junk food.

8. Although there is an increase concern with junk food and obesity, candy sales continue to increase. Today the United States has a $23 billion candy market..

9. Over 500 million Twinkies are made and produced by hostess each year.

10. The agent that gives Twinkies their smooth feel, cellulose gum, is also used in rocket fuel to give it a slightly gelatinous feel.

11. Cracker Jack was the first to use toys to target children and originated in Chicago. During the 1930s, extruded snacks

were invented by an animal feed technician, Edward Wilson, whose Korn Kurls, an early precursor to Cheetos, became popular after WWII.

12. A Children's Food Campaign (CFC) survey found that some baby food has as much, if not more, saturated fats and sugar as junk food.

13. Western diets often include snacking on junk food filled with sugar. Consequently, insulin remains high throughout the day, which can cause metabolic problems including type 2 diabetes. Over 250 million people worldwide have type-2 diabetes, constituting more than 90 percent of global diabetes cases. Most people will eventually become disabled or die from the disease.

14. Doughnuts most likely originated in Germany and were brought to New York by Dutch settlers who called them *olykoeks* (oily cakes). The hole in the center was developed by the Pennsylvania Dutch perhaps because the shape provided easier dunking in coffee or made it easier to fry the donuts more thoroughly. Dunkin Donuts sells 6.4 million donuts per day (2.3 billion per year).

15. Annually, Americans buy nearly $2 billion in Easter candies, including 90 million chocolate Easter bunnies, 16 billion jellybeans, and 700 million marshmallow Peeps.

16. For 3,000 years, natural licorice was used as medicine to treat ulcers, sore throats, coughs, and other diseases. The first licorice "candy" was an attempt to disguise the bitter flavor of the medicine, though now most American licorice "candy" does not have licorice's historic therapeutic qualities.

17. Corn dextrin, a common thickener used in junk food, is also the glue on envelopes and postage stamps.

18. Alloxen, a byproduct of bleaching white flour which is often found in junk food, leads to diabetes in healthy experimental animals by destroying their pancreatic beta cells.

19. M&M's were created by Forrest Mars (the son of the founder of Mars, Inc.) and his business partner, Bruce Murrie (the son of the president of the Hershey Company). Because both

their last names started with "M," they called their new candy M&M's. The original colors were red, yellow, green, orange, brown, and violet.

20. Snickers are the most popular candy bar in America, due in part to advertising that highlighted its healthful aspects. In the UK, Snickers was renamed Marathon Bar because "snickers" rhymes with "knickers," a British colloquialism for someone's underwear.

21. Mars, Inc, claims that the 3 Musketeers bar was named after its original composition: three pieces and three flavors: vanilla, chocolate, and strawberry. When the price of strawberries rose, the company dropped them as an ingredient in the chocolate bar.

22. The Tootsie Roll is named after its creator Leo Hirschfield's daughter Clara, whose nickname was Tootsie. It was the first penny candy that was individually wrapped. During WWII, Tootsie Rolls were placed in soldiers' ration kits because it could survive various weather conditions.

23. Young women who eat a junk food diet are at a higher risk for developing Polycystic Ovarian Syndrome (PCOS).

24. The Twinkie derived its name after bakery manager Jimmy Dewar saw an advertisement for the "Twinkle Toe Shoe Company" on a trip to St. Louis in the 1920s. They became the best selling snack cake in the United States after WWII and have appeared in many movies such as *Ghostbusters* (1984), *Grease* (1978), and *Sleepless in Seattle* (1993).

25. "Conversation hearts" started in the 1860s, and currently the New England Confectionery Company (NECCO) produces about 8 billion Sweethearts per year, all within the six weeks before Valentine's Day.

26. The creamy middle of a Twinkie is not cream at all but mostly Crisco, which is vegetable shortening.

27. In 1891, William Wrigley Jr. began selling soap in Chicago. To increase sales, he gave away gum to his customers. When his gum became a hit, he decided to make and sell the now popular gum, which was later included in rations for soldiers.

28. The most popular cookie in America is the chocolate chip cookie, which is attributed to Ruth Wakefield circa 1933.

29. Junk food became a part of the American diet during the 1920s, but it was through television advertising after WWII that junk food became more ubiquitous and nutritionists subsequently became concerned.

30. Mothers who eat junk food while pregnant or breast-feeding have children who are prone to obesity throughout life. The children are also more prone to diabetes, raised cholesterol, and high blood fat.

31. Female cockroaches that ate junk food in a research study became fatter and took longer to reproduce than cockroaches that ate a healthier diet.

32. Researchers suggest that breast cancer rates in China are rising because of an increase in Western-style junk food and increasing unhealthy lifestyles.

33. Additives and preservatives such as common food dyes and sodium benzoate can cause children to become more hyperactive and easily distracted than usual.

34. Daily candy and junk food intake in children has been linked to violence later in life, though experts are not sure if it is the candy itself or the way it is given to children that creates the association.

35. Vending machines were developed in the United Kingdom in the 1880s and were used to sell gum at train stations in New York. By 1926, there was one vending machine for every 100 people in America.

36. Founded in 1927, 7-Eleven was once called Tote'm stores since customers "toted away" what they bought. In 1946, the name was changed to 7-Eleven to reflect its original hours of operation, 7 a.m. to 11 p.m. 7-Eleven now sells about 144 million Slurpees, 33 million gallons of fountain drinks, 100 million hot dogs, and 60 million donuts and pastries per year.

37. Today, Americans consume approximately 70 million "tator tots" a year. The film *Napoleon Dynamite* (2004) popularized them even more.

The Scourge of the Black Death

1. The plague epidemic swept through Europe from 1348 - 1351, killing an estimated 25–60% of Europeans. Some estimates are as high as 2/3 of the population.

2. The number of deaths varied considerably by area and depending on the source. Current estimates are that between 75 and 200 million people died from the plague.

3. During the plague, it was called "the Great Mortality" or "the Pestilence". Although the period known as the Black Death ended in 1351, the plague continued to return to Europe, with epidemics every few years through the end of the fifteenth century.

4. The Black Death was the second plague pandemic of the Middle Ages. The first, Justinian's Plague in the sixth century, was deadly and widespread, but did not create the same devastation as the second pandemic.

5. The Black Death followed a period of population growth in Europe which, combined with two years of cold weather and torrential rains that wiped out grain crops, resulted in a shortage of food for humans and rats. This caused people and animals to crowd in cities, providing an optimal environment for disease.

6. In 1346, rumors of a plague that started in China and spread throughout Asia, Persia, Syria, Egypt, and India reached Europe. All of India was rumored to have been depopulated.

7. The first named victims of the plague were Kutluk and his wife Magnu-Kelka in 1338 and 1339 in the area around Lake Issyk Kul (Lake Baikal) in Russia.

8. In 1347, during a siege of the Genoese city of Kaffa by the Tatars, the inhabitants were reportedly infected with the plague when the Tatars threw the bodies of plague victims into the city.

9. In November 1347, a fleet of Genoese trading ships landed in Messina, Sicily after trading along the coast from the Black Sea to Italy. The ships carried dead and dying sailors, many of whom had strange black growths on their necks, in their

armpits, or in their groins. Many coughed blood. Those who were alive died within days.

10. From Sicily, the disease only took three years to sweep through Europe, moving north and traveling as far as Iceland and Greenland. The plague and simultaneous climate changes put an end to the European colonies on the coast of Greenland.

11. More than half the population died in Seina. Work stopped on the city's great cathedral, planned to be the biggest in the world, and was never resumed. The unfinished structure still stands as reminder of the death that stopped construction.

12. In May 1349, the plague reached Bergen, Norway, on a ship carrying wool from England. Within days of arriving in Bergen, the crew and passengers of the ship had all died.

13. Most agree that the cause of the plague was by *Yersinia pestis* (or *Y the. pestis*), a bacillus carried by fleas that live primarily on rats and other rodents that were common in medieval dwellings.

14. Since the 1980s, several researchers have blamed other diseases, such as anthrax and typhus, for the plague. The argument claims that other diseases spread more easily between people without the required flea population and can display similar symptoms.

15. A November 2000 study of tooth pulp in a French plague grave showed the presence of *Y. pestis* in all of 20 samples from three victims.

16. *Y. Pestis* infects its flea by blocking its stomach. The flea tries to feed, but the blockage causes it to vomit bacilli into its host. When the host dies, the flea and its offspring seek a new host, infecting humans when necessary.

17. *Y. pestis* causes three varieties of plague: bubonic plague, caused by bites from infected fleas, in which the bacteria moves to lymph nodes and quickly multiplies, forming growths, or buboes; pneumonic plague, a lung infection that causes its victim to cough blood and spread the bacteria from person to

person; and septicemic plague, a blood infection that is almost always fatal.

18. The mortality rate for humans who caught the bubonic plague was 30-75%. The pneumonic plague killed 90-95% of its victims. The septicemic plague killed nearly 100% of the people it infected and still has no cure to this day.

19. Many thought the plague was a punishment from God for the sins of the people.

20. Many also believed the plague was caused by pockets of bad air released by earthquakes or by an unfavorable alignment of Saturn, Jupiter, and Mars in the 40th degree of Aquarius on March 20, 1345.

21. The sun is the closest star to Earth and is 149.60 million kilometers (92.96 million miles) away. Virtually nobody suspected the ever-present rats and fleas.

22. Even though Jews and Muslims were as likely to be infected as Christians, they were often accused of causing the plague to destroy the Christians.

23. After being tortured, some Jews confessed that they were poisoning wells and other water sources, creating the plague. As a result, Jews were expelled or killed by the thousands.

24. The entire Jewish population of Strasburg, Germany, was given the choice to convert to Christianity or be burned on rows of stakes on a platform in the city's burial ground. About 2,000 were killed.

25. Many doctors believed that bad smells could drive out the plague. As a result, some of the treatment for the disease included feces and urine, as well as other ingredients that were more likely to spread disease than to cure it.

26. Other supposed ways to prevent or cure the plague were to be happy and avoid bad thoughts, drink good wine, avoid eating fruit, put fragrant herbs in beverages, avoid lechery, do not abuse the poor, eat and drink in moderation, maintain a household in accordance with a person's status, and so on.

27. Bathing during the plague was discouraged for two reasons. First, it was a sign of vanity, which invited the wrath of God and the punishment of sin. Second, bathing was believed to open the pores, making it easier for bad air to enter and exit the body, spreading disease. The latter belief was common throughout Europe well into the nineteenth century.

28. Perfumes were often first used during the plague to cover up odors due to not bathing or changing clothing.

29. Although the poor were hit hardest, nobles often got it as well. King Alfonso XI of Castile and León was the only reigning monarch to die, but many members of royal families from England were killed.

30. Bodies were piled up inside and outside city walls where they lay until mass graves could be dug. This contributed to the bad air and helped to spread the disease.

31. Closed communities, such as monasteries and nunneries, were especially vulnerable. If one person became infected, the whole community might die. And because friars and nuns tended the sick, infection among them was common.

32. Gherardo, brother of the famous humanist Petrarch and a monk in the monastery of Montriuex, was the only survivor of the plague in his monastery, along with his dog. He buried the other 34 monks himself.

33. *Only 7 of 140 of the Dominican brothers in Montpellier* survived.

34. English soldiers carried the disease from France to England, beginning an especially devastating round of plague in England that some estimates claim killed as much as 75% of the population in many areas.

35. During the plague, music was rare and grim. Other art forms, including visual arts and literature, also reflect the misery of the time.

36. As the population dwindled and society crumbled, old rules were ignored. The Catholic Church lost influence, creating the seeds that led to Protestantism.

37. The attempts to find cures for the plague started the momentum toward development of the scientific method and the changes in thinking that led to the Renaissance.

38. After the Black Death, plague epidemics continued to ravage Europe. For example, London was struck by the Great Plague of 1665, with thousands of deaths. This plague was followed almost immediately by the Great Fire, leaving London devastated.

39. A third pandemic began in China and India in the 1890s and even reached the United States, with infections being especially dangerous in the San Francisco Bay Area. It was during this pandemic that the real cause (*Y. pestis*) was discovered, along with a cure.

40. Plague continues to survive in the modern world, with *Y. pestis* foci in Asia, Russia, the American Southwest, and other areas where the host rodents and fleas live. Today, though, it is rarely fatal.

For A Healthy Back

Staying in shape through regular stretching and exercise will help you to do the everyday outdoor chores while avoiding an aching back.

Before heading into the garden, stretch and warm up. A 10-minute walk or bike ride will warm and loosen muscles, preparing them for the work ahead.

For safety's, be sure you have good pair of gloves, a filled water bottle (drink often to avoid dehydration and its resulting headaches), knee pads, sunscreen and insect repellent.

Work at the time of day when you consistently feel your best and use the following tips to help protect your back as you garden:

Pace yourself. Rest periodically, before your muscles start to ache. Respect your body's signals of tired stiffness that tell you to change positions or take a break.

Garden chores such as raking put stress on your body. Stretching properly is essential for a strong, healthy , pain free back.

Stretches To Strengthen Your Back

You should seek doctor's approval before trying any of these stretches. We have to say that to protect ourselves from any injuries you might sustain by stretching. But having a healthy back is pertinent to alleviating future back injuries or pain. These six simple stretches can aid in a pain free back according to Dr. Michael C. Smith.

SHOULDER RETRACTION

Clasp hands behind back. Squeeze shoulder blades back and down. Feel stretch across upper chest and shoulders.

STANDING EXTENSIONS

Standing with heels of hands on lower back, gently arch backward.

ARM STRETCH

Grab the opposite elbow behind your head and pull across behind head. Repeat other arm. Feel stretch in shoulder and sides.

KNEES-TO-CHEST STRETCH

On your back with knees bent, slowly pull knees to chest. Relax and stretch back muscles. Return to starting position.

LEVATOR STRETCH

Face forward, head straight. Hold forearm behind lower back with opposite hand. Slowly bend head forward and rotate to the side.

HAMSTRING STRETCH

With both knees bent, hold behind one thigh with both hands. Straighten knee and hold.

Fast Food Facts

1. Approximately nine out of 10 American children visit a McDonald's restaurant ever month.

2. In 1970, Americans spent about $6 billion on fast food. In 2006, the spending rose to nearly $142 billion.

3. During the early 1900s, the hamburger was thought to be unsafe to eat, and food for as poor and were not served in restaurants. Street carts typically served them.

4. Proportionally, hash browns have more fat and calories than a cheeseburger or Big Mac.

5. At some fast food chains, both in U.S. and in other countries, managers are rewarded bonuses when they reduce employee wages to save money.

6. McDonald's and other fast food chains have intentionally engaged in anti-union activities to keep wages low.

7. Today, with the exception of North Korea, Coca-Cola and PepsiCo products are sold in every country in the world.

8. Late comedian and talk-show host Johnny Carson labeled the hamburger the "McClog the Artery." In 2005, the *Advertising Age* cited Ronald McDonald as the number two top-10 advertising icon of the twentieth century. The Marlboro Man was number one.

9. The Los Angeles Time printed the first located reference to the hamburger in 1934.

10. There are more than 300,000 fast food restaurants in the just in the U.S.

11. Due to anti-German sentiment during WWI, an alternative name for a hamburger (which was derived from the Hamburg steak sandwiches eaten on immigrant ships between Hamburg, Germany, and America in the 1800s) was "Salisbury steak." It was named after Dr. Salisbury who prescribed ground beef for patients suffering from anemia, asthma, and other illnesses.

12. The popularization of the automobile resulted in "flashier" fast food restaurant building to catch the attention of drivers. This lasted until the 1970s when communities began to complain about the exaggerated buildings.

13. A&W Root Beer is named after Roy Allen and Frank Wright, the founders of the company. Allen bought the recipe from a pharmacist who had perfected it for making root beer. A&W was one of the first fast food franchises.

14. Television greatly expanded its ability to reach children and try to develop brand loyalty early in life. Today the average American child sees more than 10,000 food advertisements each year on television.

15. Fast food companies, theme parks and the movie industry work together. The companies seek to promote and "product place" one another for incredible profit. For example, Frito Lay sponsors the California Screamin' roller coaster at Disneyland, and movies intentionally feature a type of fast food (e.g., Pizza Hut in *Wayne's World*).

16. *Advertising Age* selected the McDonald's slogan "You Deserve a Break Today" as the best advertising campaign of the twentieth century.

17. In 1949, Richard and Maurice McDonald opened the first McDonald's restaurant in San Bernardino, California: the McDonald Brothers Burger Bar Drive-In.

18. The largest employer in Brazil is McDonalds.

19. There was a seven mile long line of cars waiting at the opening of an McDonalds outlet in Kuwait shortly after the end of the Gulf War.

20. In 2004, PETA released a video taken at Pilgrim's Pride, a chicken supplier to fast food restaurants, which showed intense animal cruelty.

21. In 1949, Forrest Raffel and his younger brother Leroy created a restaurant that sold roast beef sandwiches. They spelled out the initials "Raffel Brothers (RB) to create the name "Arby's."

22. McDonald's initially did not want its customers to stay and socialize, they prohibited newspaper boxes, candy machines, telephones, pinball machines, jukeboxes, and other types of entertainment. They also installed uncomfortable chairs to deter customers from lingering.

23. The popularization of the drive-thru led car manufacturers in the 1990s to install cup holders in the dashboards. As fast food drinks became larger, so did the cup holders.

24. A genetically engineered hormone called rBGH is given to cows in the U.S. to increase milk production—even though its chemical byproducts may be carcinogenic. Residues of rBGH have been found in meat products, such as hamburgers sold in fast food chains.

25. Caffeine is the most commonly used drug in the world, and high doses can have serious health effects, including muscle weakness, heart irregularities, and infertility. Children and teenagers consume more than 64 gallons of soft drinks per year.

26. Carl Karcher of Anaheim, California, launched Carl's Jr in 1956. They were mini versions of the restaurant he already owned and, hence, he called them Carl's Jr.

27. Coca-Cola originally included coca derivatives such as cocaine in their sodas, which at the time was not illegal. It was originally served as a "brain tonic and intellectual soda fountain beverage."

28. Critics of fast food argue that it advocates a pernicious consumerism that destroys both the environment and health of the world. Some critics warn of "the McDonaldization of America" in which fast food chains threaten small businesses and homogenize American life.

29. The spread of E.coli and mad cow disease are just a few of the dozen examples of food-borne pathogens linked to beef. Some meatpackers have considered radiating meat to kill the bacteria in tainted meat. Some scholars also claim hamburger meat may cause Alzheimer's disease.

30. Eating fast food can result in high levels of insulin, which

has been linked to rising incidences of Type 2 Diabetes. In fact, more than 600,000 new cases of diabetes are diagnosed each year.

31. Two fast food chains claim to have opened the first drive-ins: Pig Stand, which opened in 1921 in Texas, and A&W Root Beer, which launched in California in 1919.

32. White Castle, started by J. Walter Anderson and Edgar Waldo "Billy" Ingram, is considered to be the first fast food restaurant. Its major product was a hamburger, which had been sold as sandwiches by street vendors since the 1890s.

33. Burger King's Double Whopper with cheese contains 923 calories. A man would need to walk for about nine miles to burn it off. Adding French fries and a large cola brings the total calories to an amazing 1,500 calories (2/3 of an adult man's recommended daily caloric intake).

34. The combination of French fries and hamburgers is a continuation of the "meat and potatoes" mentality that has been the core of American food since the eighteenth century.

35. When it was revealed in 1990 that McDonald's used beef tallow to flavor its French fries, Hindu vegetarian customers in Mumbai (formerly Bombay), India, ransacked a McDonald's restaurant and smeared cow dung on a statue of Ronald MacDonald.

36. French fries are the single most popular fast food in America. In 1970, French fries surpassed regular potato sales in the United States. In 2004, Americans ate 7.5 billion pounds of frozen French fries.

37. In-N-Out Burger is one of the few fast food restaurants that actually slice each potato by hand shortly before it is placed in the deep fryer.

38. When France refused to join the American-led coalition against Iraq, some Republicans argued that the name French fries be changed to "liberty fries."

39. Hamburgers are not served in India out of respect for Hindu religious beliefs, and beer is served at McDonald's in Germany.

40. The invention of the meat grinder in the mid nineteenth century gave rise to the hamburger. Currently, between 40,000 and 50,000 meatpackers, many of whom pack meat for fast food chains, are injured every year, making meatpacking one of the most dangerous jobs in the United States.

41. Among the first fast food mascots was Big Boy, a plump boy with red-and-white checkered overalls with the words "Big Boy" spread across his chest. The first McDonald's mascot was "Speedee," a little chef with a hamburger hat. McDonald's later settled on the iconic Ronald McDonald— and today 96% of American children recognize him.

42. McDonald's is the largest purchaser of beef, pork, and potatoes and the second largest purchaser of chicken in the world. Its annual orders for French fries constitute 7.5% of America's entire potato crop.

43. McDonald's is one of the largest owners of real estate in the world and it earns the majority of its profits from collecting rent, not from selling food.

44. By the end of the twentieth century, one out of eight American workers had at some time been employed by McDonald's and 96% of Americans had visited McDonald's at least once. It was also serving an estimated 22 million Americans every day and even more abroad.

45. High-fructose corn syrup (which tricks your body into wanting to eat more and to store more fat) first appeared in 1967, and the average American now consumes 63 pounds of it a year. It is ubiquitous in fast foods.

46. Dangerous fast food ingredients that have been linked to various cancers and/or obesity includes MSG, trans fat, sodium nitrite, BHA, BHT, propyl gallate, aspartame, Acesulfame-K, Olestra, potassium bromate, and food coloring Blue 1 and 2, Red 3, Green 3, and Yellow 6.

47. Burger King's Triple Whopper with cheese has an amazing 1,230 calories. Hardies Monster Thickburger has 1,420 calories and 2,770 grams of sodium. Carl's Jr.'s Double Six hamburger has 1,520 calories and 111 grams of fat. Most people need only 44-66 grams of fat per day, and most of them should come from sources like nuts, fish, and olive oil.

Going Postal

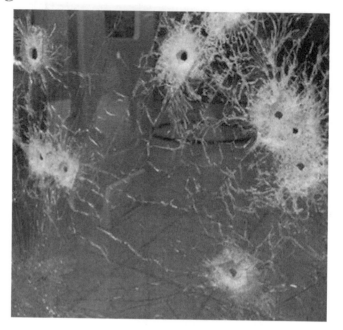

The sign on the wall says
there's bullet proof glass.
And to please get in line
behind the person whose last.

Then I got to thinking,
what that signs about.
It's not to keep bullets from coming in.
It's to keep them from coming out.

Facts Surrounding Harry Potter

Harry Potter has become a worldwide phenomenon starting from Books, then movies, then toys, and now a theme park in Florida. There are so many fun and interesting facts. Here we are just listing a few.

1. Rowling is the first person to become a billionaire by writing books.

2. Rowling says the idea of Harry Potter just "strolled into her head" during a four-hour train delay.

   Rowling claims that her wizarding world is purely imaginary and she doesn't believe in the kind of magic found in her books. (However it does now exist at Universal Florida.)

3. Harry Potter's birthday is July 31, 1980. Rowling's birthday is also July 31—but in the year 1966.

4. The make and model of Mr. Weasley's flying car is the Ford Anglia.

5. Rowling said that if she were to be a teacher in the wizarding world, she would write spell books.

6. Harry Potter's pet snowy owl is named Hedwig and shares her name with two famous saints. One is Saint Hedwig of Andechs (1174-1243), a former duchess noted for her benevolence and compassionate nature. The other is Saint Hedwig, Queen of Poland (1373-1399).

7. The headmaster of Hogwarts before Dumbledore was Armando Dippet.

8. Owls are the primary means of communication between wizards in Harry's world.

9. In *Harry Potter and the Sorcerer's Stone*, dragon blood is revealed to be an effective oven cleaner.

10. Rowling's books were the first children's books to be included on the New York Bestseller list since 1952.

11. As of 2009, Harry Potter books have sold over 500 million copies and have been translated into over 60 languages.

12. The death of Hedwig in *Harry Potter and the Deathly Hallows* represents Harry's loss of innocence and coming of age.

13. Author J. K. Rowling revealed that Dumbledore is gay and he had a crush on the wizard Grindelwald, whom he later defeated in a wizard duel.

14. The remedy to lighten the effects of a Dementor who is both magical and deadly is chocolate.

15. The name Voldemort comes from the French words meaning "fly from death," and his entire goal is to conquer death.

16. In the second Harry Potter novel, Rowling shows us that "I am Lord Voldemort" is an anagram of "Tom Marvolo Riddle," which is his actual full name.

17. Voldemort's wand is made of yew. Yew is seen by some as having immense supernatural power and being a symbol of death and rebirth, the same immortality that Voldemort seeks.

18. "Morsmorde" is the command that makes the Dark Mark (the mark of Voldemort) appear and means "take a bite out of death" in French, making it an appropriate call for Death Eaters.

19. Rowling said that when she took an online Sorting Hat quiz, it sorted her into Hufflepuff, one of the four houses of Hogwarts

20. Harry Potter's name may refer to a "potter's field," which is a cemetery in which people of unknown identity or the very poor are buried. This would be fitting because Harry Potter serves as a type of "everyman," a powerful mythological archetype.

21. Rubeus Hagrid, one of Harry's closest friends, is part wizard and part giant. *Rubeus* is Latin for something produced from a bramble or a thicket, which fits Rowling's description of him as "wild." *Hagrid* most likely comes from the term "haggard" which also means "wild" or "unruly."

22. Rowling was runner up for *Time* magazine's Person of the

Year in 2007.

23. Rowling's mother from multiple sclerosis significantly influenced her writing, and death is a major theme throughout the Potter series.

24. Rowling used "witchy" sounding names such as toadflax, goutwort, grommel, and others in *Culpeper's Complete Herbal*, a famous book of herbal text from the 1600s.

25. *Harry Potter and the Deathly Hallows* sold 11 million copies on the first day of its release.

26. The driver and conductor of the Knight Bus, Ernie and Stanley, are named after Rowling's grandfathers.

27. When *Harry Potter and the Prisoner of Azkaban* was released in Great Britain, the publisher asked stores not to sell the book until schools were closed for the day to keep kids from skipping school to get the book.

28. Several publishers rejected the first Harry Potter manuscript with excuses such as the script was too long and literary, but Bloomsbury Publisher finally accepted it in 1996.

29. The book's publisher suggested Rowling use the name "J. K." rather than her real name "Joanne Rowling" to appeal to male readers.

30. Joanne Rowling took the name added the "K" to "J.K." from her grandmother's name Kathleen, but neither "Kathleen" nor "K" is part of her legal name

31. Colors play an important role in the Harry Potter novels. For example:

    - Red represents goodness, such as Gryffindor's scarlet robes, Harry Potter's red ink, and the crimson colored Hogwarts Express train. The Weasley's have red hair and a red roof.

    - Green is associated with mainly negative events, such as when Harry sees a flash of green when his parents die and the green-colored curse that made Ron vomit.

32. Numbers 3 and 7 are symbolic in the Harry Potter series as well.

    - 3 for example makes up the trio of Harry, Ron, and Hermione suggest the power of three and the spiritual trinity. Harry fatally wounds the basilisk on its third strike, and Hagrid knocks on the front door of Hogwarts three times.

    - 7 for example is the number of years students attend Hogwarts. There are seven players on each Quidditch. Sirius is also imprisoned on the seventh floor of Hogwarts.

33. *Harry Potter and the Philosopher's Stone* refers to a mythical object called a "philosopher's stone." In the ancient practice of alchemy (from the Arabic word *al-kimia,* or the transformation of metals, and related to the word a*lgebra*), alchemists searched for a magical substance called the "philosopher's stone" that would turn ordinary metals into gold. In Harry Potter and the Philosopher's Stone, the "philosopher's stone" is described as "blood-red."

34. Rowling has said her favorite beast in the series is the phoenix which is a sacred bird who ignites into flames when it reaches 500 or 1,000 years old only to emerge from the flames as a new and young phoenix.

35. Natalie McDonald, who appeared in *Harry Potter and Goblet of Fire*, was based on a real girl Rowling knew who was dying of leukemia.

36. Cedric Diggory is one of two students to die in Rowling's novels. Cedric is a common Welsh name and Diggory is the name of professor in *The Lion, the Witch, and the Wardrobe.*

37. Rowling has said she may have inadvertently taken the name of Harry's school, "Hogwarts," from a hogwort plant in K]

38. Gardens in New York City.

39. So many fans visit King's Cross station to take pictures of platforms 9 and 10 that the station management erected a sign that says "Platform 9 ¾" which, in the Potter books, is

invisible to Muggles but acts as a gateway for witches and wizards.

40. Historically, nearly all wizards have used a magical wand of some sort that channels a wizard's power and acts a symbol of authority such as a shepherd's staff.

41. Rowling has said if she could take Polyjuice Potion for an hour, she would become Prime Minister Tony Blair.

42. Rowling has said that she would be dreadful at playing Quidditch as she is "not sporty," "not great with heights," and is "clumsy."

43. Quid ditch is also known as *Ikarosfairke* or "Ikarus ball," which refers to the Greek myth of Icarus who flew too close to the sun. His wings melted and he fell into the sea and drowned.

44. The curse used to kill Harry Potter's parents, "Avada Kedavra," derives from a phrase in Aramaic *Abhadda kedhabhra,* which means to "disappear like this word

45. Harry Potter's godfather's name, Sirius Black, comes from the name of one of the brightest stars in the sky, the "Dog Star" or Sirius from the Greek word *seirios,* meaning "burning".

46. Sirius Black's tattoos are borrowed from Russian prison gangs. The markings identify the person as someone to be feared and respected.

47. Albus Wulfric Percival Brian Dumbledore is Dumbledore's real full name.

48. Dumbledore is an Old English word meaning "bumblebee."

49. Albus is Latin for "white."

50. Wulfric was the name of a twelfth-century saint who became a deeply holy man after seeing a homeless man in the street.

51. Percival was a knight of King Arthur's Round Table and may also mean "pierce the veil,"

52. Brian is a Celtic name, meaning "strong."

53. The original title of the first book was *Harry Potter and the Philosopher's Stone* and appeared on books in the United Kingdom, Canada, Australia, and other territories. It was changed to *Harry Potter and the Sorcerer's Stone* by the American publisher because "Sorcerer's" seemed more exciting.

54. The Death Eaters were originally known as the Knights of Walpurgis, which is a reversal of "Walpurgis Night," the name of an old witch's holiday on April 30th which is 6 months from Halloween.

55. Saint Walpuriga was actually the name of a nun who lived between A.D. 710-779.

56. Harry Potter books made the American Library Association (ALA) list of 100 Most Frequently Challenged Books for five consecutive years. A challenge is a formal, written complaint filed with a library or school requesting that materials be removed because of content or appropriateness.

57. Nancy Stouffer, the author of *The Legend of Rah and the Muggles* and *Harry Potter and His Best Friend Lilly* sued Rowling because she said Rowling's books were based on her ideas. Stouffer lost her case in 2002 and was fined for making her case with knowingly forged documents.

58. The Hogwarts school motto is *Draco dormiens nunquam titillandus* which is Latin for "Never Tickle a Sleeping Dragon.".

59. Hogwarts was founded 1,000 years ago by Godric Gryffindor (fire/lion), Salazar Slytherin (water/serpent), Helga Hufflepuff (earth/badger), and Rowena Ravenclaw (air/raven). Its crest includes each of the animal representations of the four founders.

60. In the Hogwarts School, grades include Outstanding, Exceeds Expectations, and Acceptable. The failing grades include Poor, Dreadful, and Troll.

61. In the novels, the school is located somewhere in Scotland and has various charms to make it appear as an old ruin to

muggle eyes.

62. A lice outbreak among the children cast members occurred while filming *Harry Potter and the Chamber of Secrets*.

63. When Coca-Cola won the rights to tie in its product with *Harry Potter and the Sorcerer's Stone*, Rowling required the company to donate $18 million to the U.S. Reading Is Fundamental campaign.

64. A theme park called the Wizarding World of Harry Potter opened in 2010 at Universal Islands of Adventure in Florida. The park will include a Hogwarts School of Witchcraft and Wizardry, the Forbidden Forest, and Hogsmeade Village.

Common Androgynous Names

For years one of our editors has been collecting a list of names which can be given to both a boy or a girl. This all started when she became pregnant and wanted to wait until the baby was born to give the baby a name. Well friends and family started to ask what the baby would be named. To help solve the problem, she and her husband began a list of names which could be used regardless of the sex of the baby. They picked one from the list. Over the years they kept up the list on every new name they found. Here are the results.

Boy Names	Girl Names
Adrian	Adrian
Billy	Billie
Bobby	Bobbi
Cameron	Cameron
Carey	Kerry
Carol	Carol
Carter	Carter
Charlie	Charlie
Chris/Kris	Chris/Kris
Claude	Claude
Cory	Cori
Dana	Dana
Daryl	Daryl
Desi	Desi
Don	Dawn
Drew	Drew
Francis	Francis
Gene	Jean
Jackie	Jackie
Jay	Jaye
Jerry	Jeri/Gerry
Jesse	Jesse
Jimmy	Jimi
Jody	Jodi

Boy Names	Girl Names
Johnny	Jonny/Joni
Jordan	Jordan
Kay	Kay
Kelly	Kelly
Kim	Kim
Lindsey	Lindsay
Loren/Lauren	Loren/Lauren
Lou	Lou
Lupe	Lupe
Lyn	Lynn
Pat	Pat
Randy	Randi
Riley	Riley
Robin	Robin
Ronny	Ronni
Sean/Shawn	Shawn/Sean
Shannon	Shannon
Sonny	Sonny
Stacey	Stacey
Stevey	Stevie
Taylor	Taylor
Terry	Terri
Tony	Toni
Tracey	Tracy
Tyler	Tyler

Men and Women

Making Him Work for a Date

Recently I met a girl who makes any man she meets write a list of 99 reasons why she should date him. This one was amusing and forced a reply from her. We published both.

1. My shoelaces are hardly ever untied.

2. I don't pick his nose in public.

3. Have never put a new red shirt in with the whites.

4. I rarely stand on a swivel chair to reach a high shelf.

5. When getting off an elevator at a 20+ story building, I don't push all the buttons so everyone has to stop at every floor.

6. Elvis is dead and Bob Saget is married; who's left?

7. Reads National Geographic, and not just for the nude pictures of African gorillas.

8. I seldom turn the volume on my stereo up sufficiently to shake the neighbors' walls.

9. I haven't wet the bed for at least two weeks now

10. I have never been responsible for starting a war, or even a border dispute.

11. Always keeps his printer paper well-stocked.

12. Doesn't turn into a werewolf during full moons.

13. I have never played a mean trick on Smokey the Bear. I rarely stare directly at the sun.

14. I will administer chocolate whenever you feel the need.

15. I'm willing to supply cold milk, warm backrubs, and hot baths. In other words: all temperature cheer.

16. I'm the best there is at what I do.

17. I'm not really obnoxious, just tact-impaired.

18. Played no part in the Cuban Missile Crisis.

19. I am smarter than a computer. I can count past 1.

20. I make excellent use of my spare time. You're reading what I do.

21. I have an imagination, and I don't mind using it.

22. I intend to live forever. So far so good.

23. I mix up 'dessert' and 'desert' less and less every day.

24. I have never found rude shapes in clouds.

25. My face has never appeared on an FBI wanted poster.

26. I occasionally stumble across the truth.

27. I am a member of Dogbert's New Ruling Class.

28. Never have I failed a quest given me by a King.

29. I rarely employ multi-megaton warheads for insect control.

30. You intrigue me.

31. I wears male undergarments (not G-strings)

32. I have never been struck by lightning while simultaneously being hit by a falling meteorite

33. I am an accomplished TV-watcher

34. I am fully functional.

35. I have never opened fire on an innocent group of unarmed people.

36. Did not mastermind Julius Caesar's death; that was Cassius.

37. I lift heavy objects with a straight back and my knees bent.

38. I regularly get the high score on "Super Mario Bros." if there are no other players.

39. I have never dumped in his pants while sliding into 2nd base.

40. I only *look* innocent.

41. When I jump into the air, I always remember to come down again.

42. I am new and improved.

43. I subscribe to the theory that the earth is round.

44. So far I have never resorted to cannibalism.

45. I have never once thought of exploiting the tradition of mistletoe to kiss anyone. Until I met you.

46. I never stare at someone's wart for more than 2-3 minutes.

47. I have scanned my PC for viruses.

48. I have never stepped in a bear trap.

49. I have no communicable diseases. I cannot say the same about my computer.

50. There is seldom any doubt that I am human.

51. I have very little trouble remembering where I live.

52. I'm all-natural, no artificial colors or flavors.

53. Nothing ventured, nothing gained.

54. I am the culmination of millions of years of random mutations.

55. I am cleverly disguised as a responsible adult.

56. I have never gambled away a girlfriend in Las Vegas, as well as many other places in the world.

57. Gets fewer and fewer 'ice-cream headaches' (Brain freezes)

58. I am trustworthy. (re: Boy Scout Handbook - Scout Laws)

59. I am loyal. (re: Boy Scout Handbook - Scout Laws)

60. I am helpful. (re: Boy Scout Handbook - Scout Laws)

61. I am friendly. (re: Boy Scout Handbook - Scout Laws)

62. Contrary to popular belief, does not comb his hair with a fork.

63. I never pile up old magazines or newspapers where they could be a fire hazard.

64. I always proofread carefully to see if I any words out. ☺

65. It's been over a year since he last got his neck tangled in a telephone cord.

66. I can sing "Frere Jacques" much better than Jean-Luc Picard.
    A cheap thrill is still a thrill.

67. Usually remembers to take the shell off of an egg before eating it.

68. I am weird enough for most purposes.

69. I have never poured soap into a swimming pool or fountain.

70. I'm user-friendly.

71. Unlike Vincent Van Gogh, I would not chop off his ear for a girl.

72. There are few things in life more important than friends.

73. I have made mistakes, but I'm a stronger person because of it.

74. I know how to perform the Heimlich Maneuver.

75. Rarely do I take candy from strangers.

76. I know the capital of New York.

77. I always make sure I have sufficient personal flotation devices aboard any pleasure boat I am using.

78. As of yet, has never overlooked the importance of regular, continuous breathing.

79. I deny reality whenever possible.

80. If you don't go out with me, you'll feel bad about it in the morning.

81. Occasionally, I have been known to have a clue.

82. Try it, you'll *like* it.

83. I never put off until tomorrow what I can put off indefinitely.

84. I can take a lickin' and keep on tickin'.

85. I'm available.

86. I have had all my shots.

87. I own my own body, but I share.

88. I am alive, occupying space, and exerting gravitational force.

89. I'm not afraid to cry - admittedly it's usually when I hurt myself, but I can build on that.

90. I know the difference between a woofer, a midrange and a tweeter.

91. I have never once burned an egg while trying to boil it.

92. I rarely ever forget a phone number or my password to my online banking.

93. I am usually on time for dates.

94. I can think of something different to do on each of our first 99 dates.

95. I really think you're awesome.

96. I really want to know you better.

97. I really want to go out with you.

98. I am really convincing.

99. Now give me 99 reasons why you should date me.

The Reply from a Girl – 99 Reasons to Date Me

1. Cats seem to like me.
2. I have never landed a light aircraft on the Whitehouse lawn.
3. Nor have I landed a light aircraft near the Kremlin.
4. I believe the rabbit should be given some Trix.
5. I hardly ever slurp when drinking soup.
6. If you let me take you to dinner, you get free food.
7. I give good back rubs.
8. I'm a good listener.
9. Dating me is much more fun than hitting yourself on the head with a hammer.
10. I have never broken into a bear's home and eaten all his porridge.
11. I have no communicable diseases.
12. I'm cuddly.
13. I always resist the urge to poke sharp objects into my ear on the first date.
14. I am persistent.
15. As of yet, I have never overlooked the importance of regular, continuous breathing.
16. I can usually eat spaghetti without getting sauce on my shirt.
17. I have never pulled the football away from Charlie Brown.
18. My shoelaces are hardly ever untied either.
19. The rumors of my involvement in the Chernobyl crisis are mostly unfounded.
20. I can, at the touch of a button, have a pizza delivered to me in 30 minutes or less.
21. I don't cry over spilled milk.
22. I give great foot rubs when asked.
23. I have never locked myself in a car.

24. I would never smoke nor drink while pregnant. Or ever.

25. I'm really a nice person once you get to know me.

26. I always shave my legs before a social occasion. I am an accomplished TV-avoider.

27. I like to fly kites.

28. I am not an alien from another dimension bent on world domination.

29. I can sympathize with you about how high-heeled shoes feel if you ever decide to wear them.

30. I seldom pick a fight with inanimate objects.

31. I believe that every person has the potential to become great.

32. I feel that reading a good book is an excellent way to spend time.

33. I practice random acts of kindness.

34. I always remember to use pixie dust when attempting to jump out of a window and fly. Just kidding.

35. I change my toothbrush when the blue color-bristles go away.

36. I feel that a relationship can exist without sex if it needs to.

37. I would never wear black shoes with a blue skirt.

38. You'll forever wonder what you're missing if you don't date me. Trust me.

39. I'm not *that* much of an eyesore.

40. I take a bath or shower at least once a day.

41. I have not been proven to cause holes in the ozone Layer.

42. I'm housebroken.

43. As hard as it may to believe, I have never lost a pole-vault competition. (I've never been in one either.)

44. I have never hit a silver-medalist in the knee with a club while ice skating.

45. Stop judging by mere appearances, and make a right judgment. (John 7:24 NIV)

46. I don't turn into a werewolf during a full moon.

47. I seldom eat crackers in bed.

48. I am usually able to find Waldo.

49. I am heterosexual.

50. I have never committed a violent crime.

51. To everything there is a season, and a time to every purpose under the heaven. (Ecc. 3:1 KJV) Therefore, you will eventually go out with me. *smile*

52. I am excellent at compiling purposeless lists like this.

53. The possibility exists that I am more fun in person than your computer.

54. I have never gotten into a tug-of-war with a marine platoon.

55. When I wash my nylons, I don't leave them hanging in the bathroom after they're dry.

56. If you don't like me, I promise to give you a full refund.

57. Nobody can heat up a TV dinner better than I can.

58. I don't use "pet names" for body parts.

59. I do my own laundry.

60. The voices in my head told me you would like me. *smile*

61. I do not drink and drive. (At least not alcohol. Sprite, maybe.)

62. You'll never get a collect call from me.

63. Dating me will be a life-enriching experience.

64. I have never played a part in any oil spills in any gulf region of the world.

65. There is a refreshing absence of monsters under my bed lately. I sure miss them. Just kidding.

66. I have never caused a bunny to tear the buttons off his jacket while he was trying to escape from my garden.

67. My blender has never had a frog in it.

68. There's no compelling reason why you shouldn't date me.

69. I can change a flat tire while wearing a skirt and heels.

70. Just do it!

71. I recycle my aluminum cans and plastic bottle regularly.

72. I am anxious to find someone to share my hopes, dreams, and wishes with.

73. I seldom get my teeth stuck together when eating a Jolly Rancher candy.

74. I had no part in the extinction of either the dodo or the passenger pigeon.

75. I have never yelled "Fire!" in a crowded theatre.

76. Dating me is more fun than doing your income taxes.

77. I have never tried to convince Henny-Penny that the sky is falling.

78. I understand the difference between their, there, and they're.

79. I was nowhere near the grassy knoll on November 3rd, 1963. Actually I wasn't even conceived yet.

80. I think Nancy Drew is a better detective than the Hardy Boys.

81. I'll supply you with chocolate chip cookies.

82. I have no plans to give the Pope a wedgie.

83. I have never been a telemarketer.

84. I am faster than an unfired bullet.

85. I can leap tall housecats in a single bound.

86. I am gainfully employed.

87. I check the expiration date on my milk carton before I drink it.

88. I have never caused a traffic accident because I was fixing my makeup.

89. I usually remember to take the shell off an egg before eating it.

90. I have gotten to the Tootsie-roll center of a Tootsie-Pop without biting.

91. We are of opposite genders in the same species.

92. Extensive research has proven that I am, indeed, a carbon based life form.

93. I occasionally practice senseless acts of beauty.

94. I can have it my way at Burger King.

95. I am hardly ever referred to as 'infernal'.

96. I use my seat belt.

97. It would make me smile.

98. It might make you smile too.

99. I usually answer my phones voicemails in 30 minutes or less. So call me for a date.

I Would Never Trade My Friends

I would never trade my amazing friends, my wonderful life, my loving family for less gray hair or a flatter belly. As I've aged, I've become kinder to myself, and less critical of myself. I've become my own friend. I don't chide myself for eating that extra chocolate chip cookie, for not making my bed, for buying that silly plate for my wall that I didn't need, but looks so great on my wall. I am entitled to a treat, to be messy, and to sometimes be extravagant.

I have seen too many dear friends leave this world too soon; before they understood the great freedom that comes with aging.

Whose business is it if I choose to read or play on the computer until 4 AM and sleep until noon? I will dance with myself to those wonderful tunes of the 70 & 80's, and if I, at the same time, wish to weep over a lost love ... I will and always remember them.

I will walk the beach in a swim suit that is stretched over a bulging body, and will dive into the waves with abandon if I choose to, despite the pitying glances from the younger audience.

They, too, will get old.

I know I am sometimes forgetful. But there again, some of life is just as well forgotten. And I eventually remember the important things.

Sure, over the years my heart has been broken. How can your heart not break when you lose a loved one, or when a child suffers, or even when somebody's beloved pet gets hit by a car? But broken hearts are what give us strength and understanding and compassion.

A heart never broken is pristine and sterile and will never know the joy of being imperfect.

I am so blessed to have lived long enough to have my hair turning gray, and to have my youthful laughs be forever etched into deep grooves on my face.

So many have never laughed, and so many have died before their hair could turn silver.

As you get older, it is easier to be positive. You care less about what other people think. I don't question myself anymore. I've even earned the right to be wrong.

So, to answer your question, I like being old. It has set me free. I like the person I have become. I am not going to live forever, but while I am still here, I will not waste time lamenting what could have been, or worrying about what will be. And I shall eat dessert every single day(if I feel like it).

-Anonymous Thoughts

Everything You Need To Know About A Simple Kiss

On average you will spend an estimated 20,160 minutes kissing in your lifetime but here are some things you might also like to know.

1. 50% of people have their first kiss before they are 14.

2. The word "Kiss" is from the Old English *cyssan* from the proto-Germanic *kussijanan* or *kuss*, which is based on the sound kissing can make.

3. Kissing can help reduce tooth decay because the extra saliva helps clean out your mouth.

4. You burn 26 calories a minute kissing.

5. The science of kissing is called philematology.

6. On average a human will spend up to 2 weeks kissing in his/her lifetime.

7. The insulting slang "kiss my ass" dates back at least to 1705.

8. Lips are 100 times more sensitive than the tips of the fingers. Not even genitals have as much sensitivity as lips.

9. Approximately two-thirds of people tip their head to the right when they kiss.

10. It is illegal for a man with a moustache to "habitually kiss human beings" in Indiana

11. It is illegal for a man to kiss his wife on a Sunday in Hartford, Connecticut.

12. The most important muscle in kissing is the *orbicularis oris,* also known as the kissing muscle, which allows the lips to "pucker."

13. French kissing involves all 34 muscles in the face. A pucker kiss involves only two.

14. The lips of resemble the lips of the vagina.

15. The term "French kiss" came into the English language around 1923 as a slur on the French culture which was thought to be overly concentrated on sex. In France, it's called a tongue kiss or soul kiss because if done right, it feels as if two souls are merging. In fact, several ancient cultures

thought that mouth-to-mouth kissing mingled two lovers' souls.

16. The Four Vedic Sanskrit texts (1500 B.C.) contain the first mention of a kiss in writing.

17. The Roman culture there are three categories of kissing: (1) *Osculum*, a kiss on the cheek, (2) *Basium*, a kiss on the lips, and (3) *Savolium*, a deep kiss.

18. Passionate kissing burns 6.4 calories a minute. A Hershey's kiss contains 26 calories, which takes five minutes of walking–or about four minutes of kissing–to burn off.

19. It is possible for a woman to reach an orgasm through kissing.

20. Some scholars speculate that the way a person kisses may reflect whether he or she was breast fed or bottle fed.

21. Scientists believe that kissing may be a way of exchanging body salts or sebum that form relationships with parents and lovers, just as it does some birds. During mating, some birds chew food, then kiss-feed it to a prospective mate. If a bird's sebaceous glands are removed so there is no sebum, its mate flies off.

22. The anticipation of a kiss increases the flow of saliva to the mouth, giving the teeth a plaque-dispersing bath.

23. A medieval manuscript warns Japanese men against deep kissing during the female orgasm because a woman might accidentally bite off part of her lover's tongue.

24. The *Kama* (desire) *Sutra* (type of verse) lists over 30 types of kisses, such as "fighting of the tongue."

25. According to one study, many men are more particular about which women they kissed than who they went to bed with, suggesting that kissing is somehow more about love than sex is.

26. Kissing may have originated when mothers orally passed chewed solid food to their infants during weaning. Another theory suggests kissing evolved from prospective mates sniffing each others' pheromones for biological

compatibility.

27. Scholars are unsure if kissing is a learned or instinctual behavior. In some cultures in Africa and Asia, kissing does not seem to be practiced.

28. Common chimpanzees kiss with open mouths, but not with their tongues. Bamboos, the most intelligent of primates, do kiss with their tongues.

29. Leper-kissing became fashionable among medieval ascetics and religious nobility during the twelfth and thirteenth centuries. It was deemed proof of humility.

30. During the middle ages, witches' souls were supposed to be initiated into the rites of the Devil by a series of kisses, including kissing the Devil's anus, which was a parody of kissing the Pope's foot.

31. Pliny insists that kissing a donkey's nostril will cure the common cold.

32. Kissing at the end of a wedding ceremony can be traced to ancient Roman tradition where a kiss was used to sign contract.

33. The first on-screen kiss was shot in 1896 by the Edison Company. Titled *The May Irwin-John C. Rice Kiss*, the film was 30 seconds long and consisted entirely of a man and a woman kissing close up.

34. The first on-screen kiss between two members of the same sex was in Cecil B. DeMille's 1922 *Manslaughter*.

35. Under the Hays Code (1930-1968), people kissing in American films could no longer be horizontal; at least one had to be sitting or standing, not lying down. In addition, all on-screen married couples slept in twin beds...and if kissing on one of the beds occurred, at least one of the spouses had to have a foot on the floor.

36. the kiss between Ingrid Bergman and Cary Grant in the 1946 film *Notorious* is one of the sexiest kisses in cinematic history. Because the Hays Code allowed on-screen kisses to last only a few seconds, Alfred Hitchcock directed Bergman

and Grant to repeatedly kiss briefly while Grant was answering a telephone call. The kiss seems to go on and on but was never longer than a few seconds.

37. *Don Juan* (1926) is known as the movie with the most kisses in which John Barrymore and Mary Astor share 127 kisses. The film with the longest kiss is Andy Warhol's 1963 film *Kiss*. The 1961 film *Splendor in the Grass*, with Natalie Wood and Warren Beatty, made history for containing Hollywood's first French kiss.

38. Early Christians kissed one another in highly specific settings that distinguished them from non-Christian population. The earliest Christian reference to the ritual kiss is at the end of I Thessalonians: "Greet one another with a holy kiss." The Christian ritual kiss or "kiss of peace" was used during prayer, Eucharist, baptism, ordination, and in connection with greeting, funerals, monastic vows, and martyrdom.

39. Kissing played an important role in ancient Greco-Roman culture and was seen as a sign of respect, thanks, reunion, and agreement, as well as a rite of inclusion. Kisses were exchanged between peers, political leaders, teachers, and priests. Hence, the kiss of Judas ("Kiss of Death") to betray Christ inverted the very point of kissing in this early Christian context.

40. In 1929, anthropologist Bronislaw Malinowski visited the Trobriand Islands to observe their sexual customs. He found that two lovers will go through a several phases of sucking and biting in a variation of the French kiss that culminates in biting off each other's eyelashes. In fact, in the South Pacific, short eyelashes are a status symbol.

41. Diseases which can be transmitted through kissing include mononucleosis ("kissing disease") and herpes. Contraction of HIV through kissing is extremely unlikely, though one woman was infected in 1997 when the woman and infected man both had gum disease. Transmission was likely through the man's blood and not his salvia.

42. Rodin's famous statue *The Kiss* was originally titled *Francesca*

da Rimini and depicts the thirteenth-century woman in Dante's *Inferno* who falls in love with her husband's younger brother Paolo. Their lips do not actually touch, hinting at their eventual doom.

43. Because the kiss of life (breath of God) and the kiss of death (Judas' kiss) are powerful literary and artistic symbols, Sixteenth century authors used them a lot as sexual metaphors.

44. Cunnilingus is a type of sexual kissing where a person stimulates the external female genital organs with the mouth or tongue. The word "cunnilingus" derives from the Latin *cunnus* (vulva, vagina) and *lingua* (tongue) or *lingere* (to lick up).

45. When two people kiss, they exchange between 10 million and 1 billion bacteria.

46. "X"s at the end of a correspondence letter represent the contact of the lips during a kiss.

Before Your Propose To Her

Before you pop the big questions, you might want to read this section first.

1. Know Her Answer.

   Many couples haven't even discussed the subject of marriage. If you've had serious discussions about your relationship and where it's headed, then you probably already know that her answer will be 'yes'. If not, don't rush out and buy a ring. Instead, drop hints here and there to see how she responds.

2. Ring Shopping.

   Get an idea of what she likes first, you don't want her hating her engagement ring. If she doesn't care about a surprise, then take her out to browse. If you want to surprise her, ask her friends and keep away from the subject. You may also want to bring along one of her current rings with you in order to get the sizing right. This ring represents your love and commitment to her, but she's the one wearing it for the rest of her life.

3. After learning her likes and dislikes, study up on the 4c's. Most men know little about diamonds. Never fear, check out this guide to the 4c's (carat, cut, color, clarity) for tips on buying a diamond.

4. Insure the Ring.

   After buying the rock, call your insurance agent and add it to your home owner's or renter's policy. Usually the fee is quite small and it will protect your investment if anything should ever happen to it.

5. Ask for Permission.

   Many men will ask their future father-in-law for their girlfriends' hand in marriage. Although this rarely happens today and isn't a requirement, it still shows respect and thoughtfulness if you ask for her father's blessing. Invite him out to dinner and let him know how much you truly love his daughter and that you'd like his blessing in asking her to marry you.

6. Be Creative.

   You only propose once, so make it memorable. Plan early and think creatively. Pick a location that holds a special place in your relationship. Be detail-oriented from the lighting to the mood. Remember that the first thing everyone will ask is 'How did he propose?'. Give her a moment to share for a lifetime. If you're stumped for ideas, check out our marriage proposal ideas with hundreds of ideas to get the creative juices flowing.

7. Get down on one knee.

   Nothing is more romantic that the man you love down on one knee, with a ring in hand, asking for your hand in marriage. Definitely makes it more memorable for her.

8. Capture the moment.

   Have a video camera set up or a friend nearby to take pictures. She'll be so surprised and excited that she won't be thinking about preserving the memory. If you've planned ahead, you'll be able to treasure the moment forever.

9. Don't be afraid to ask for help.

   If needed, get a close friend or family member to help you with the preparations. It makes the planning easier, especially if you're planning a more extravagant proposal. If nothing else, they're available for moral support. Be careful who you choose though. Pick those that you trust and make sure they keep their mouths shut

   Surprise!

   If she's like most women, she wants a surprise proposal! Even if she helped pick out the ring or knows that you've been planning to propose, you can still surprise her. Be creative and plan the proposal when she least expects it.

10. Celebrate!

    Be sure to bring your cell phone along! An engagement is such an exciting time and the first thing your fiancé will want to do is call her friends and family. After you've shared the excitement of the moment with your nearest and dearest, it's time to celebrate! Enjoy a romantic dinner, share a bottle of wine, or go all out with an engagement party.

Read This Before You Get Married

Before you get married, here are some things you MIGHT want to know.

1. The term "marriage" derives from the Latin word *mas* meaning "male" or "masculine."

2. The earliest known use of the word marriage in English dates from the thirteenth century.

3. The average couple spends only four minutes a day together. Due to jobs, kids, TV, the Internet, hobbies, home and family responsibilities. Not including sleeping.

4. The Talmud is very strict about banning extramarital sex—but also enforcing marital sex. The Talmud even lays out a timetable for how often husbands should "rejoice" their wives. For men of independent means, every day; for laborers, twice a week; for ass-drivers, once a week; for camel-drivers, once in 30 days; and for sailors, once in six months.

5. Over 75% of people who marry partners from an affair eventually divorce.

6. The Oneida colony established in New York in 1848 advocated "complex" or group marriage in which every woman was married to every man. They also practiced "scientific breeding" where parents where matched by a committee according to physical and mental health.

7. Traditionally, bridesmaids would be dressed in similar bride-like gowns to confuse rival suitors, evil spirits, and robbers.

8. Marrying younger than age 25 dramatically raises the divorce risk. Also, the divorce risk is higher when the woman is much older than the man, though the reverse isn't as a strong factor.

9. The average married couple has sex 58 times per year, or slightly more than once a week.

10. At Italian weddings, it is not unusual for both the bride and groom to break a glass. The number of shards will be equal

to the number of happy years the couple will have.

11. The word "wife" is likely from the Proto-Indo-European root *weip* ("to turn, twist, wrap") or *ghwibh*, which has a root meaning "shame" or "pudenda."

12. The word "husband" is from the Old Norse *husbondi* or "master of the house" (literally, *hus* "house" + *bondi* "householder, dweller").

13. Some scholars trace the word "bride" to the Proto-Indo-European root *bru*, "to cook, brew, make broth."

14. The term "groom" is from the Old English *guma*, meaning "man."

15. In three states—Arkansas, Utah, and Oklahoma—women tend to marry younger, at an average age of 24. Men's average age is 26. In the northeastern states of New York, Rhode Island, and Massachusetts, men and women wait about four years longer to marry. The U.S. average age for women is 25.6 and for men, 27.7.

16. A person's level of education influences the age at which they marry. Couples tend to marry later in states with higher numbers of college-educated adults, while the opposite is true for states with lower education levels.

17. Nevada, Maine, and Oklahoma have the highest percentage of divorced adults. Arkansas and Oklahoma have the highest rates of people who have been married at least three times.

18. The probability of a first marriage ending in a divorce within 5 years is 20%, but the probability of a premarital cohabitation breaking up within 5 years is 49%. After 10 years, the probability of a first marriage ending is 33%, compared with 62% for cohabitations.

19. Hammurabi's Code (ca. 1790 B.C.), an ancient Babylonian law code, contains some of the oldest known and recorded marriage laws. These early laws defined marriage as a contract that paradoxically served to protect women and restrict them. According to the Code, a man could divorce his wife if she could not bear children or of she was a

"gadabout" who humiliated her husband in public and neglected her house. Additionally, she could be "pitched" in a river if she committed adultery.

20. Washington, D.C., has the lowest marriage rate in the nation.

21. Approximately $6 billion in revenue is lost by American businesses as a result of decreased worker productivity linked to marriage hardship. Employees in a happy marriage, in contrast, tend to increase a company's bottom line.

22. CNN reports that the current economy is the biggest stress on married couples in the past 60 years.

23. A *New Woman's Day* and *AOL Living* poll found that 72% of women surveyed have considered leaving their husbands at some point.

24. Married couples tend to have fatter waistlines, which can lead to a decrease in sexual attraction and general health. Additionally, a spouse's chances of becoming obese increase by 37% if his or her partner is obese.

25. A 2008 study found that marital satisfaction improves once children leave home. However, if marital problems existed before, an empty nest often reveals those otherwise masked issues.

26. People whose marriage has broken down at the time they are diagnosed with cancer do not live as long as cancer patients who are widowed, have strong marriages, or who have never been married.

27. In ancient Greece, Solon (638-538 B.C.) once contemplated making marriage compulsory, and in Athens under Pericles (495-429 B.C.), bachelors were excluded from certain public positions. In Sparta, single and childless men were treated with scorn. In ancient Rome, Augustus (63 B.C.-A.D. 14) passed drastic laws compelling people to marry and penalized those who remained single.

28. A marriage ceremony typically ends with a kiss because in ancient Rome, a kiss was a legal bond that sealed contracts,

and marriage was seen as a contract.

29. Adults who are childhood cancer survivors are 20-25% less likely to marry compared with their siblings and the general American population.

30. Stress associated with divorce affects the body's immune system and its ability to fend off the disease. The health benefits of remarriage are reduced the second and third times around.

31. Throughout most of history, marriage was not necessarily based on mutual love, but an institution devoted to acquiring in-laws and property and to provide the family additional labor forces (by having children).

32. A white New Orleans man in the late nineteenth century transfused himself with blood from a black woman he loved so he could overcome anti-discrimination laws by claiming he was black and marry her.

33. One nineteenth-century New York legislator insisted that letting married women own their own property attacked both God and Nature.

34. Just two years after marriage, an estimated 20% of couples make love fewer than 10 times in a year.

35. One in three American marriages is "low sex" or "no sex."

36. The number of marriage therapists in the United States has increased 50-fold between 1970 and 1990.

37. In the United States, over 50% of first marriages end in divorce, 67% of second marriages end in divorce, and nearly 74% of third marriages end in divorce.

38. Marriage does more to promote life satisfaction than money, sex, or even children, say Wake Forest University psychologists.

39. Compared to singles, married people accumulate about four times more savings and assets. Those who divorced had assets 77% lower than singles.

40. Married elderly people are more likely to maintain daily

health-promoting habits, such as exercising, not smoking, eating breakfast, and having regular medical check-ups.

41. More than friendship, laughter, forgiveness, compatibility, and sex, spouses name trust as the element crucial for a happy marriage.

42. Eighty-one percent of happily married couples said their partner's friends and family rarely interfered with the relationship, compared to just 38% of unhappy couples.

43. Eighty-five percent of couples have had premarital sex.

44. Nearly 60% of married adults have had at least one affair.

45. The cost of an average wedding is $20,000. The cost of an average divorce is $20,000.

46. Words form only 7% of our communication with anyone, including spouses. Tone of voice accounts for 38% and body language is responsible for 55% of the messages spouses receive from each other.

47. Women who report a fair division of housework were happier in their marriages than women who thought their husbands didn't do their fair share. Wives also spent more quality time with their husbands when they thought the housework was divided fairly.

48. A 15-year-long study found that a person's happiness level before marriage was the best predictor of happiness after marriage. In other words, marriage won't automatically make one happy.

49. Researchers found a huge decline in happiness four years into a marriage with another decline in years seven to eight. In fact, half of all divorces occur in the first seven years of marriage, which gives rise to the popular term "the seven-year itch."

50. More than two in five Catholics marry outside their church, twice as many as in the 1960s. There are at least one million Jewish-Christian marriages in the U.S. Two in five Muslims in America have chosen non-Muslim spouses.

51. Married people are twice as likely to go to church as

unmarried people.

52. Half of emotional affairs become sexual affairs.

53. While couples with children are less likely to divorce than childless couples, the arrival of a new baby is more likely to bring more stress and emotional distance than new happiness. Nearly 90% of couples experienced decrease in martial satisfaction after the birth of their first child.

54. Over 40% of married couples in the U.S. include at least one spouse who has been married before. As many as 60% of divorced women and men will marry again, many within just five years.

55. Birth order can influence whether a marriage succeeds or fails. The most successful marriages are those where the oldest sister of brothers marries the youngest brother of sisters. Two firstborns, however, tend to be more aggressive and can create higher levels of tension. The highest divorce rates are when an only child marries another only child.

56. The number of men and women age 65 and older cohabiting outside of marriage nearly doubled between 1990 and 2000.

57. Because Virginia law required an ex-slave to leave the state once freed, one freed woman petitioned the legislature in 1815 to become a slave again so she could stay married to her still-enslaved husband.

58. For many centuries, the Catholic Church argued that contraception was a sin and made the wife no better "than a harlot." Up until 1930, many Protestant churches agreed.

59. One seventeenth-century Massachusetts husband was put in stocks alongside his adulterous wife and her lover because the community reasoned she wouldn't have strayed if her husband had been fulfilling is marital obligations.

60. Research points to certain characteristics that are most often linked to infidelity, such as being raised in a family where having affairs is considered normal, having a personality that values excitement and risk taking over marital stability, having coworkers and friends who believe affairs are

acceptable, and feeling emotionally distant from one's spouse.

61. No sex in a marriage has a much more powerful negative impact on a marriage than good sex has a positive impact.

62. Modern Western marriage traditions have long been shaped by Roman, Hebrew, and Germanic cultures as well as by doctrines and traditions of the Medieval Christian church, the Protestant Reformation, and the Industrial Revolution.

63. Levirate marriage, where a man is obligated to marry his brother's widow if she had no sons to care for her, is sometimes required in the Bible (as in Deuteronomy) and sometimes prohibited (as in Leviticus).

64. The first recorded mention of same-sex marriage occurs in Ancient Rome and seems to have occurred without too much debate until Christianity became the official religion. In 1989, Denmark was the first post-Christianity nation to legally recognize same-sex marriage.

Tips for a Long Happy Marriage

Have you ever wondered "what is the secret to a long and happy marriage?" Our collection of tried and true marriage advice tips will help you answer that very question! These secrets to a happy marriage come straight from the horse's mouth -- those who are happily married!

1. Never assume anything.
2. Compliment more than you criticize.
3. For everything negative u vent about your husband/wife to your friends, tell three positive stories.
4. Remember that it is ok to do things.
5. Always make time for each other.
6. Marry someone that you enjoy listening and talking to.
7. Remember that marriage is a bed of roses and sometimes there are thorns.
8. Remember that the best gift that you can give your children is to love their mother/father.
9. Split the housework, spending money, etc evenly. This way you are never resentful of your partners contributions (or lack of) or expenditures.
10. Never go to bed angry.
11. Remember that it's normal for people to fight. It's how you do it that matters.
12. Pick your battles. Before starting an argument, consider if it's really worth it.
13. Fight naked. It hard to argue with a naked person.
14. Never, ever mention the "D" word (divorce).
15. Do you want to be right all the time or do you want to be married?

16. Respect each other's privacy. Even though you're married, people still need there space.

17. Marriage is not 50/50, its two people giving 100/100 all of the time.

18. Show the love. Surprise each other now and then.

19. The real secret to a long happy marriage is two TV's!

20. Set aside some time. Have date night!

21. Never pass up an opportunity to say "I love you".

22. Just because your married doesn't mean u can't hold hands.

23. Hug & kiss every day (several times a day actually!).

24. Always believe that you got better than you deserved.

25. Be quick to say "I'm sorry".(even if u think it's not your fault)

26. Choose the one you love, then love the one you choose.

27. Keep the in-laws out of your marriage!

28. Love isn't always a feeling, it's a decision.

29. Hang in there. It's worth it.

30. Play nice, play often, love much.

31. Never air your dirty laundry as a couple in public.

32. Never keep secrets from each other.

33. No matter what, take your husband or wife's side first!

33. Communication is the key!

34. Always respect each other.

35. Never underestimate the power of a good laugh and don't be afraid to laugh at yourself.

36. It's the little things that matter most.

37. Never use the words 'Always' and 'Never' in a fight.

38. It's ok to argue, but never use curse words to express your anger.

39. Never compare your marriage to others. What you see on the outside is not always what it is on the inside.

40. Don't make love in the same place or position every time. Variety is the spice of life!

Facts You Might Reconsider when Getting Pregnant

1. If you are pregnant, you are not alone. Because each year in the United States, there are approximately six to seven million pregnancies. This means that at any one time, about 4-5% of women in the U.S. are pregnant.

2. Only about 25% of couples actively trying to conceive will experience pregnancy within the woman's first cycle. However, 90% of couples will achieve pregnancy within the first 12 months of actively trying.

3. Approximately 10% of pregnancies will end in miscarriage. Many miscarriages often occur before a woman even knows she is pregnant.

4. Each year, 1.2 million women in the U.S. choose to end their pregnancies through early termination.

5. About 3% of all pregnant women will give birth to twins. This rate is an increase of nearly 60% since the early 1980s. However, 17% of pregnant women over 45 will give birth to twins.

6. Nigeria has the highest twinning rate in the world at around 4.5%. Some experts attribute this number to the large consumption of yams in Nigeria.

7. Just fewer than 500,000 babies are born each year in the U.S. to teenage mothers.

8. After delivery, approximately 13% of U.S. women are diagnosed with post-partum depression.

9. The average size of a full-term baby in the U.S. is 8 pounds. This is an increase from an average size of 6 pounds 30 years ago.

10. The largest baby ever born weighed in at over 23 pounds but died just 11 hours after his birth in 1879. The largest surviving baby was born in October 2009 in Sumatra, Indonesia and weighed an astounding 19.2 pounds at birth.

11. Less than 1% of women in the United States choose to deliver their babies at home, while 30% of Dutch women

opt for home births.

12. Approximately one in three babies in the United States is now delivered by cesarean section. The number of cesarean sections in the U.S. has risen nearly 46% since 1996.

13. According to a *Time Magazine* article published in 1945, the longest pregnancy on record is 375 days (as opposed to the usual 280 days). Amazingly, the delivered baby was only 6 pounds, 15 ounces.

14. The highest number of surviving children from a single birth is eight with Californian Nadya Suleman giving birth to octuplets in January 2009. The octuplets were made up of six boys and two girls and celebrated their first birthday on January 26, 2010.

15. Fewer than 10% of babies are born on their exact due date, 50% are born within one week of the due date, and 90% are born within two weeks of the date. Pregnant women at a healthy weight should eat an extra 300 calories per day. This amount is roughly equivalent to a serving of yogurt and half of a bagel.

16. While not all pregnant women will crave pickles and ice cream specifically, pregnancy cravings are rooted in the body's extra need for minerals and comfort-inducing serotonin.

17. Despite several rumors to the contrary, microwave ovens do not pose a threat to an unborn fetus.

18. During pregnancy, a woman is more likely to experience bleeding gums and nosebleeds due to hormonal changes that increase blood flow to the mouth and nose.

19. Milk production and lactation can actually begin as early as the second trimester in some women. Carrying a baby "high" or "low" is dependent on a woman's body type and is not a reliable predictor of the baby's gender.

20. Approximately 70% of expectant mothers report experiencing some symptoms of morning sickness during the first trimester of pregnancy.

21. Pregnant women usually experience a heightened sense of smell beginning late in the first trimester. Some experts call this the body's way of protecting a pregnant women from foods that are unsafe for the fetus.

22. Many women experience thicker and shinier hair during pregnancy due to hormonal changes and consumption of extra vitamins. New hair volume gained during pregnancy typically begins to fall out after three months post partum.

23. While the feet do not actually get longer or wider during pregnancy, most women do gain up to half a shoe size, due to increased fluid volume in the foot.

Facts About...Women

1. The word "woman" is believed to have derived from the Middle English term *wyfman*, broken down simply as the wife (*wyf*) of man. In Old English, women were described simply as *wyf*, while the term *man* was used to describe a human person, regardless of gender.
2. The English word "girl" was initially used to describe a young person of either sex. It was not until the beginning of the sixteenth century that the term was used specifically to describe a female child.
3. The biological sign for the female sex, a circle placed on top of a small cross, is also the symbol for the planet Venus. The symbol is believed to be a stylized representation of the Roman goddess Venus' hand mirror.
4. While many stars and moons are christened with female names, Venus is the only planet in our solar system given the name of a female goddess.
5. The English language originally delineated between women in different stages of life with the terms "maiden," "mother," and "crone." A maiden referred to a young girl who was unmarried, a mother referred to a woman in her child-bearing years, and a crone described a post-menopausal woman.
6. The average height of a woman in the U.S. is approximately 5 feet 4 inches, and the average weight is about 163 pounds. These figures vary greatly throughout the world, due to differences in nutrition and prenatal care.
7. In almost every country worldwide, the life expectancy for women is higher than for men.
8. While the population of males is slightly greater than females worldwide (98.6 women for every 100 men), there are roughly four million more women than men in the U.S. In the age 85-and-older category, there are more than twice as many women as men currently living in the U.S.
9. The most common cause of death for American women is heart disease, which causes just over 27% of all mortalities in females. Cancer ranks just below, causing 22% of female

deaths.

10. Worldwide, women are nearly twice as likely to be blind or visually impaired as men. Experts attribute this difference to the greater longevity of women (leading to more age-related visual impairment) and specific eye diseases that are intrinsically more common in women such as dry eye syndrome and Fuch's Dystrophy.

11. Depression is the most common cause of disability in women, and approximately 25% of all women will experience severe depression at some point in their lives.

12. Over 90% of all cases of eating disorders occur in women, and nearly seven million women in the U.S. currently suffer from anorexia nervosa or bulimia.

13. Approximately one in five women worldwide reports being sexually abused before the age of 15.

14. About 14 million adolescent girls become pregnant each year, with over 90% of those girls living in developing countries.

15. It's sad. Almost 1,600 women a die each day from child birth complications. Almost 99% of these deaths occur in developing nations.

16. Approximately 95% of all women in the U.S. have been married at least once by the age of 55.

17. Of the 154.7 million women currently living in the U.S., nearly 83 million are mothers.

18. The probability of a woman giving birth to a baby girl instead of a baby boy increases significantly the nearer the mother lives to the equator. While the cause of this gender selection is unknown, scientists believe the constant sunlight hours and abundant food supply in tropical regions may favor female births.

19. Approximately 5.6 million women in the U.S. reported themselves as stay-at-home moms in a 2007 census report

20. The first Mother's Day was held on May 10, 1908, and was organized by Anna Jarvis in West Virginia and Philadelphia. As the event gained popularity throughout the country, Congress designated the second Sunday in May as a national day of recognition for mothers in 1914.

21. International Women's Day is held each year on March 8.

The annual event was first observed worldwide in 1909.

22. In the U.S., Congress established a national week of recognition for women's history in 1981. This recognition, held during the second week of March, was later expanded into a full month by a congressional resolution in 1987. The month of March is now designated as National Women's History Month.

23. According to a 2007 Census Bureau report, one-third of American women aged 25 to 29 have earned a bachelor's or advanced college degree.

24. More American women work in the education, health services, and social assistance industries than in any other industry. These three industries employ nearly one-third of all female workers.

25. Women in the U.S. labor force currently earn just over 77 cents for every one dollar men earn.

26. Approximately 14% of active members in the U.S. armed forces today are women. In 1950, women comprised less than 2% of the U.S. military

27. The first woman to run for U.S. president was Victoria Woodhull, who campaigned for the office in 1872 under the National Woman's Suffrage Association. While women would not be granted the right to vote by a constitutional amendment for nearly 50 years, there were no laws prohibiting a woman from running for the chief executive position.

28. The first female governor of a U.S. state was Wyoming governor Nellie Tayloe Ross, elected in 1924.

29. Wyoming was the first state to give women the right to vote, enacting women's suffrage in 1869.

30. The first country to grant women the right to vote in the modern era was New Zealand in 1893.

31. The first woman to rule a country as an elected leader in the modern era was Sirimavo Bandaranaike of Sri Lanka, who was elected as prime minister of the island nation in 1960 and later re-elected in 1970.

32. Women currently hold 17% of Congressional and Senate seats and 18% of gubernatorial positions in the U.S.

33. According to an ancient Sumerian legend, the universe was

created by a female, the goddess Tiamat. This role of a female creator is not unique, as the Australian Aboriginal creation myth also credits the creation of life to a woman.

34. The earliest recorded female physician was Merit Ptah, a doctor in ancient Egypt who lived around 2700 B.C. Many historians believe she is the first woman recorded by name in the history of all of the sciences.

35. A person's gender is biologically determined by the sex chromosomes, one set of a human's 23 pairs of chromosomes. Women have two X chromosomes, while men have one X and one Y chromosome.

36. The world's first novel, *The Tale of Genji*, was published in Japan around A.D. 1000 by female author Murasaki Shikibu.

Facts about Men

1. In Old English, human men were referred to as *wer*, while the term *man* was used to describe humanity as a whole. During the thirteenth century, *man* gradually replaced *wer* as the term for an adult human male while also maintaining its use as an expression for the entire human species.

2. Worldwide, there are approximately 107 baby boys born for every 100 baby girls. Scientists believe the elevated birth rate in favor of boys may be linked to the higher mortality rates of boys in infancy and childhood.

3. Globally, boy babies are 25% more likely to die in infancy than girl babies.

4. In the U.S the average height for a man is just over 5' 9" (175 cm) and average weight is approximately 190 pounds (86 kg). In 1960, average height for men was about 5' 8" (172 cm) and average weight was just over 166 pounds (75 kg).

5. Worldwide, men have a life expectancy of 64.52 years, as the average for woman is 68.76 years.

6. The most common cause of death for men in the U.S. is heart disease (the same as for women), and the average age of a first heart attack for men is just 66 years.

7. In the U.S., men have higher death rates for all of the 15 leading causes of death (with the exception of Alzheimer's disease) and on average die more than five years younger than women.

8. The adult male brain is about 10% larger in total size than the brains of women. Because men generally have a larger stature and more muscle mass than women, their brains require more neurons to control the body.

9. Scientists have discovered that men and women's brains actually function somewhat differently. When focused on a task, men tend to use only one side of their brain at a time, devoting all of their attention and concentration to the task

at hand. Women, on the other hand, tend to use both sides of the brain at the same time, making them more adept at "multi-tasking."

10. The word "boy" has been in use since 1154 A.D. as a descriptive term for a male child. The exact etymology of the word is unclear, but it is believed to have descended from the Anglo-Saxon word boia, meaning "servant" or "farm worker."

11. Boys typically experience puberty between the ages of 12 and 14, a time in which the voice changes to its lower timbre, growth spurts occur, and the secondary sex characteristics begin to develop. Puberty for boys generally occurs later than in girls of

12. Both boys' and girls' voices will change during puberty, the change in a boy's voice is dramatic, sometimes dropping a whole octave in tone. Males in other species develop a deeper voice to attract females and intimidate other males, and scientists believe the change in the male human voice evolved for the same reasons.

13. The "Adam's apple," or laryngeal prominence in the neck, is a feature primarily unique to adult men and is a result of the growth of the larynx during puberty. The term is derived from the Biblical account of Adam eating the forbidden fruit in the Garden of Eden.

14. In most cultures throughout the world, boys historically experienced a rite of passage that marked their transition into adulthood. Examples of traditional rites of passage include the "vision quest" in many American Indian tribes, and circumcision rites in many African cultures.

15. Approximately 56% of boy babies born in the U.S. are circumcised at birth, representing a decline of 20% since 1950. Worldwide, approximately one-third of men have been circumcised.

16. In terms of absolute size and in proportion to overall body mass, the human penis is longer and thicker than that of any other primate.

17. For approximately the first six weeks after conception, all human embryos develop as a default female child, primarily taking genetic information from the mother's DNA. After the sixth week of development, if the embryo is male, the SRY gene on the Y chromosome will begin to produce androgens, primarily testosterone, that encourage the development of male characteristics and inhibit the further development of female characteristics.

18. The biological symbol for the male sex, a circle with a small arrow protruding from it, is also the symbol for the planet Mars. The two components of the symbol are designed to represent the shield and spear of Mars, the Roman god of war.

19. Boys are three times more likely to be diagnosed with autistic spectrum disorders than girls. While experts do not yet have a solid answer for the obvious gender discrepancy, some believe that girls with mild autism may be better able to mask their symptoms and thus go undiagnosed.

20. Teenage boys are four times more likely than girls to drop out of school and represent more than 75% of the children referred to special education in the U.S.

21. Boys are approximately three times more likely to be diagnosed with attention deficit disorder (ADD) or attention deficit and hyperactivity disorder (ADHD) than girls are.

22. Men currently represent an even 50% of the U.S. workforce, but they account for 94% of all on-the-job fatalities.

23. Prior to the 1900s, male nurses were far more common than female nurses in nearly every country in the world. In current times, men now make up only 5.4% of registered nurses in the U.S. and only 13% of new nursing students in the now-female-dominated field.

24. Men are nearly three times more likely than women to abuse alcohol and twice as likely to abuse recreational drugs like marijuana and cocaine.

25. Higher levels of testosterone in boys and men generally cause greater levels of aggression, competition, self-assertion, and self-reliance than in women. In addition, the amygdala (the part of the brain involved in producing emotion) is typically larger in males, resulting in more aggressive, uncontrollable emotions.

26. According to the U.S. Department of Justice, men are four times more likely than women to be murdered and 10 times more likely to commit murder. Both female and male offenders are more likely to target male victims.

27. In nearly every country in the world, men are more than twice as likely to commit suicide than women. In some countries (such as Russia and Brazil), suicide rates among men are up to six times higher than those for women.

28. The average adult male has about 50% more muscle mass and 50% less body fat than the average adult female.

29. Of the more than 151 million men currently living in the U.S., approximately 64.3 million are fathers.

30. The word "dad" entered the English language in the sixteenth century and is believed to have originated from the Welsh word *tad*, meaning father. The word "father" comes from the Old English term *faeder* and was first used in the 1500s.

31. According to a 2008 estimate, there are approximately 140,000 stay-at-home fathers in the U.S. who are the primary caretakers for their children while their wives work outside the home.

32. The first Father's Day celebration in the U.S. was held on June 19, 1910, in Spokane, Washington, and was put together by Sondra Dodd. After listening to a Mother's Day sermon in 1909, Dodd wished to have a day of recognition for her father as well. Father's Day became a nationally celebrated holiday in 1972 when the third Sunday in June was designated by public law as a day of recognition for fathers.

100 Ways to Tell Someone You Care About Them

Ever run out of positive things to say to someone. Here is a list to help you.

1. You are awesome!
2. I am infatuated with you.
3. I appreciate you.
4. I can't live without you.
5. I can't stop thinking about you when we're apart.
6. I cherish you.
7. I dream of you.
8. I live for our love.
9. I love being around you.
10. I need you by my side.
11. I need you.
12. I respect you.
13. I value you.
14. I want a lifetime with you.
15. I want you.
16. I worship you.
17. I yearn for you.
18. I'm a better person because of you.
19. I'm blessed to have you in my life.
20. I'm devoted to you.
21. I'm fond of you.
22. I'm lost without you.
23. I'm nothing without you.
24. I'm passionate about you.
25. I'm thankful for you.
26. I'm yours.
27. Me and you. Always.

28. My love is unconditional.

29. Our love is invaluable.

30. Take me, I'm yours.

31. The thought of you brings a smile to my face.

32. Ti tengu cara (to female)

33. Ti tengu caru (to male).

34. Together, forever.

35. We were meant to be together.

36. You are a blessing in disguise.

37. You are an angel from God.

38. You are like a candle burning bright.

39. You are my crush.

40. You are my dear.

41. You are my everything.

42. You are my heart's desire.

43. You are my life.

44. You are my one and only.

45. You are my one true love.

46. You are my reason for living.

47. You are my strength.

48. You are my sunshine.

49. You are my treasure.

50. You are my world.

51. You are precious.

52. You are the light of my life.

53. You are the reason I'm alive.

54. You bring happiness to rainy days.

55. You bring joy to my life.

56. You cast a spell on me that can't be broken.

57. You complete me.

58. You drive me wild.

59. You fill me with desire.

60. You fill my heart.

61. You give me wings to fly.

62. You had me from hello.

63. You hold the key to my heart.

64. You inspire me.

65. You intoxicate me.

66. You lift me up to touch the sky.

67. You light my flame.

68. You light up my life.

69. You make me hot.

70. You make my heart skip a beat.

71. You make my world a better place.

72. You mean the world to me.

73. You motivate me.

74. You rock my world.

75. You seduce me.

76. You set my heart on fire.

77. You simply amaze me.

78. You stole my heart.

79. You sweeten my sour days.

80. You turn my world upside down.

81. You turn the darkness into light.

82. You're a dream come true.

83. You're a gem.

84. You're a twinkle in my eye.

85. You're absolutely wonderful.

86. You're all I want.

87. You're as beautiful as a sunset.

88. You're beautiful.

89. You're charming.

90. You're enchanting.

91. You're heavenly.

92. You're my angel.

93. You're my perfect match.

94. You're one in a million.

95. You're priceless.

96. You're sexy.

97. You're the apple of my eye.

98. You're the best thing that ever happened to me.

99. You're the diamond in the rough.

I'm so glad I Am a Man

I'm glad I'm a man, you better believe.
I don't live off of yogurt, diet coke, or cottage cheese.
I don't complain to my girlfriends about the size of my breasts.
I can get where I want to - north, south, east or west.
Along with not worrying my chest is flat,
I don't worry at all or continually ask "Do you think I am fat?"
I don't spend hours deciding on what to wear.
Or change my wardrobe five times before I get there.
And I don't go around looking for mirrors to check my hair
or spend an hour and half to make it look good, so people will stare.
I don't whine in public and make us leave early,
and when you ask why get all bitter and surly.
I'm glad I'm a man, I'm so glad I could sing.
I don't have to sit around waiting for someone to give me a ring.
I don't gossip about friends or stab them in the back.
I don't carry our differences back to the shack.
I'll never go psycho and threaten to kill you
or think every guy out there's trying to steal you.
I'm rational, reasonable, and logical too.
I know what the time is and I know what to do.
And I honestly think it's a privilege for me
to be able to stand up when I pee.
You shouldn't get mad or get a big frown,
hey I like the seat up, but you want it down.
I live to watch sports and play all sorts of ball.
It's more fun than dealing with women after all.
I won't cry if you say it's not going to work.
I won't remain bitter and call you a jerk.
Yes, I'm so very glad I'm a man, you see.
I'm glad I'm not capable of child delivery.
I don't get all witchy every 28 days.
I'm glad that my gender gets me a much bigger raise.
I'm a man by chance and I'm thankful it's true.
I'm so glad I'm a man and not a woman like you!

***

I'm so glad I Am a Woman

I'm glad I'm a woman, yes I am.
I don't live off of video games, sports, soda's, and Spam.
I don't brag to my buddies about my erections.
I won't drive forever before I ask for directions.
I don't get wasted at parties, and act like a clown.
And I know how to put the toilet seat down.
I won't grab your breasts or pinch your butt.
My belt is not hidden beneath my big gut.
And I don't go around "re-adjusting" my thing,
Or tell all my friends I' a stud and a king.
I don't belch in public, I don't scratch my behind.
I'm a woman you know, just not that kind.
I'm glad I'm a woman, I'm so glad I could sing.
I don't have a front and a back like shag carpeting.
It doesn't grow from my ears or cover my back.
When I lean over you can't see four inches of crack.
And what's on my head doesn't leave with my comb.
I'll never allow fish or antlers to be hung in my home.
Or take tweezers to pull the grey from each side.
I'll just die it, I have too much pride.
And I honestly think it's a privilege for me,
To have these large breasts and to squat when I pee.
I don't live to play golf or watch football.
Or play video games until the sun falls.
I won't tell you my wife just does not understand,
or stick my hand in my pocket to hide the wedding band.
Or tell you a story to make you sigh and weep,
or spend two minutes with you at night, roll over and fall asleep.
Yes, I'm so very glad I'm a woman, you see.
I don't pay for nights out, you men do it for me.
I don't long for male bonding, I don't cruise for chicks.
Join the Hair Club for Men, or hit balls with long sticks.
I'm a woman by chance and I'm thankful, it's true.
I'm so glad I'm a woman and not a man like you!

***

A Mother's Letter To Santa

Dear Santa,

I've been a good mom all year. I've fed, cleaned, and cuddled my two children on demand, visited the doctor's office more than my doctor, sold sixty-two cases of candy bars to raise money to plant a shade tree in the school playground, and figured out how to attach nine patches onto my daughter's girl scout sash with staples and a glue gun.

I was hoping you could spread my list out over several Christmas', since I had to write this one with my son's red crayon, on the back of a receipt in the laundry room between cycles, and who knows when I'll find anymore free time in the next eighteen years.

Here are my Christmas wishes:

I'd like a pair of legs that don't ache after a day of chasing kids (in any color, except purple, which I already have) and arms that don't flap in the breeze, but are strong enough to carry a screaming toddler out of the candy aisle in the grocery store. I'd also like a waist, since I lost mine somewhere in the seventh month of my last pregnancy.

If you're hauling big ticket items this year, I'd like a car with fingerprint resistant windows and a radio that only plays adult music; a television that doesn't broadcast any programs containing talking animals; and a refrigerator with a secret compartment behind the crisper where I can hide to talk on the phone.

On the practical side, I could use a talking daughter doll that says, "Yes, Mommy" to boost my parental confidence, along with one potty-trained toddler, two kids who don't fight, and three pairs of jeans that zip all the way up without the use of power tools. I could also use a recording of Tibetan monks chanting, "Don't eat in the living room" and "Take your hands off your brother", because my voice seems to be out of my children's hearing range and can only heard by the dog. And please, don't forget the Play-Doh Travel Pack, the hottest stocking stuffer this year for mothers of preschoolers. It comes in three fluorescent colors guaranteed to crumble on any carpet and make the Inlaws' house seem just like home.

If it's too late to find any of these products, I'd settle for enough time to brush my teeth and comb my hair in the same morning, or the luxury of eating food warmer than room temperature without it being served in a Styrofoam container.

If you don't mind I could also use a few Christmas miracles to brighten the holiday season. Would it be too much trouble to declare ketchup a vegetable? It will clear my conscience immensely. It would be helpful if you could coerce my children to help around the house without demanding payment as if they were the bosses of an organized crime family; or if my toddler didn't look so cute sneaking downstairs to eat contraband ice-cream in his pajamas at midnight.

Well, Santa, the buzzer on the dryer is ringing and my son saw my feet under the laundry room door and wants his crayon back. Have a safe trip and remember to leave your wet boots by the chimney and come in and dry off by the fire so you don't catch cold. Help yourself to cookies on the table, but don't eat too many or leave crumbs on the carpet.

Oh, and one more thing Santa, you can cancel all my requests if you can keep my children young enough to believe in you.

--Author Unknown

The Best of Craiglist.com for 2009-2010

Unemployed Broke Girl Seeks Same for Friendship Maybe More

In an effort to appease my best friend I am finally posting a personal ad on Craigslist. I have tried explaining to her that I don't currently have a whole lot to offer a potential mate. She scoffs and informs me that I am a great person and that I should at least make an effort. Here it is. This is my effort:

I am an unemployed single female seeking a fun guy for friendship and maybe more. I don't want to feel like a leech, desperately clinging to a guy with a fancy schmancy office job (complete with health insurance!) because he can pay for things. I want an equal. A true partner. Being unemployed and broke together as opposed to apart will probably help to boost our self-esteem.

Don't worry about taking me anywhere fancy on our first date. I completely understand that the best you can do is inviting me to your studio apartment for some Ramen. I won't mind at all that we sit on orange crates and that an empty cable spool is our table. I will gladly stand on one foot with one foil wrapped hand tightly gripping your television antenna as my other arm reaches towards the window so that we can watch a very scratchy Simpsons rerun. I totally understand that you can't afford cable right now. Don't worry, I can't either!

If things go well, perhaps we'll have a second date. This time, you can come over to my place. Don't get any ideas though. Remember, neither one of us can afford condoms. I'll make you Ramen and after we're done eating we can search under my couch cushions for change. Maybe we'll come up with enough to buy a piece of gum from the gas station across the street. We'll have to split it though, because I'm not sure that there is enough change for two double bubbles in my couch.

Don't worry about running out of activities just because we're both broke and unemployed. There are plenty of things that we can do together that don't cost any money at all:

- Use my neighbor's internet connection to cruise craigslist's "free stuff" for items that we might be able to sell on eBay.
- Steal toilet paper from public restrooms when we can't afford to buy any.
- Go for walks.
- Go for more walks.
- Have competitions to see who lost the most weight last week when they couldn't afford any food.
- Offer to clean people's windshields at gas stations for the tip.
- I'm sure you can think of even more!!!

About two weeks before the end of every month I will expect you to sit on street corners with me as I pathetically attempt to make up rent money buy "playing" the guitar. (If you actually know how to play the guitar, I'll definitely write you back!)

If you happen to get a job while I am still unemployed, don't worry. It will be quick and painless to break up with me. I'll feel really crappy about no longer being equal to you and in order to cheer me up you can take me out for a few drinks. Due to the lack of food in my stomach, it will only take about two beers for me to get completely shit-faced and start crying about how I don't want to lose you to your co-workers and asking "who will sit with me on street corners now!?" While I am in this dependent and pathetic state you can take me back to my apartment and finally sleep with me (using the condoms you just bought with your first paycheck). Slip out the door after I pass out and never call me again.

I won't try to call you back. After all, by then my phone will have been completely shut off due to lack of payment.

All I ask is that if you ever see me on the street corner, still trying to figure out how to play my guitar, leave a dollar in my hat.

I am eager and excited to find my new (albeit temporary) partner!

Your pic gets mine!

Your Librarian Hates You

You never have your library card, and then you cough on me while explaining that you don't even have an ID on you.

You refuse to learn to use the computers for yourself, and get impatient when I don't know your yahoo password.

You stare blankly as I check in your 40 books so you can pay a five-cent fine.

You contest a five-cent fine.

You call me "dear" and "doll" and "sweetie".

You physically turn my computer monitor around to watch my screen if I'm helping you. Appalling.

You want to know why we don't order the paperbacks you want, after the ten letters you've written to our superiors.

You refuse to ever, ever, ever buy a book.

You angrily explain you need this book more than other people do, as you are in a prestigious "book club".

You are over sixty and compliment my eyes/smile, and wink.

You smell worse than the garbage that keeps you warm.

You put out your cigarette on your way in.

You light your cigarette in the lobby on the way out.

On good days you smell like actual vodka rather than scope.

You rearrange the items on my desk.

You pick up the book you saw me put down to assist you, and start to read.

You are banging on the door to get in, so you can save 50 cents on the newspaper.

You cut up the newspaper.

You steal the newspaper. We only have one newspaper you know.

You want a particular book a friend recommended, but you don't know the title or author or year of publication, and your friend has recently passed on.

You say anything other than "no shit, right?" when you catch me yawning.

..Such as "are we BORING YOU?"- The answer is, yes.

You let your child scream for more than 30 seconds without escorting him out.

Your stroller needs WD40.

When your child starts hysterically bawling, and we don't have to look at a clock to know it is precisely 11am. take him to the friggin park.

Your computer starts making a beeping noise because of your disk, so you just leave it for us to figure out. You play dumb: we are on to you. Your disk has your name on it, nut job.

You state loudly that librarians shouldn't have piercings. They shouldn't be on their desks after-hours either, I suppose?

You believe that being ancient means you can be a jerk wod.

WE NEED A SMART PERSON

We need a smart or more person to help un with our Company.

Jealous, controlling 300gb high-speed USB 2.0 hard disk

I've long since upgraded from this *unique* Buffalo 300gb USB 2.0 external hard disk, and now my loss can possibly be yours, too. I bought this disk around 2005, and it was amazingly massive at the time. What wonderful times we had! Happily storing and retrieving everything I sent over her 480mbit/sec high-speed USB 2.0 link, and me happily accessing it at later dates. But as time went on, my eye turned outwards. There were so many newer, prettier hard drives out there.

I admit it, I dallied. I bought a 250gb portable drive - I rationalized it. It was smaller than this one. I only needed it for when I went out. I'd always come home to my faithful Buffalo. Emboldened by this success, I became quite the rake. First came a pair of identical 500gb Seagate twins, then their younger cousin, a 500gb portable. No matter how much I had, my wanton lust for storage would not be quenched. I became irresponsible, and was known to have immodest flings. I once bought quite a tart of a 1tb disk. I spent the day with her, then returned her to the shop in the morning.

Meanwhile, the Buffalo faithfully put up with it. And then, she started exhibiting some disturbing inconsistencies. I would plug her in, dutifully waiting for the icon to appear on my desktop. I'd wait, and wait, and wait. I sometimes waited for hours or days, peering at my desktop with slavish attention, groveling for access to my miserable data. She was showing me who was really in control here, and exerting its power. I wanted to leave, but it wouldn't let me. Every time I thought about it, I'd remember all the good times we had - and more importantly, my data, which it jealously guarded.

The end came unexpectedly for her, though I planned it long in advance. I spent a full two weeks sweet-talking. I put her back in a prominent position on my desk, letting the other disks know who my favorite was. We wined and dined, and I showered her with chocolate and roses. One evening, after a particularly romantic night out at Ruth's Chris, I politely asked for access to my files. And she complied and opened right up.

I rushed in and plundered every miserable byte, leaving her magnetic surfaces a desolate, empty expanse.

Things haven't been the same between us. They never can be. Despite all our time together, good and bad, it's time to set her free. I hope you treat each other better than we did.

My guy is Cheating on me with X-Box 360

Ok, I know I'm not perfect. Nobody is. But seriously, I try really hard to be a good girl-friend. I don't send endless, paranoid texts messages to Mr. Guy (as I will refer to him), will try anything in bed - seriously, I've never said no to anything with him, and I have never mentioned "meeting the parents," "our future" or even said, "Could you help me with my car?" Nada. I almost always insist on us paying our own way at dinner or movie - look, we're both broke and I'm not looking for handouts. Plus? I HATE chic-flicks more than any guy, so as a girl friend? I would say I am above average.

Yet, despite all this, Mr. Guy decided to break the bond we shared once X-Box 360 moved into his roommate's house. Suddenly, lying in bed at midnight, I'm thinking he's going to go in for the kiss, but NO! He whispers in my ear, "One more round of Modern Warfare and I'll be back up. You just rest here."

I wake up alone hours later, sneak downstairs and find him making violent thumb war love to the X Box controls, rapidly touching that controller in a way he never did me - super sensitively, but with a firm control. ARG! Screw you, X Box 360 WHORE!

At first I thought, a couple weeks and the fascination will end. It's a new toy, he is a BOY, and... it's Seattle. I think the term "geek-out" came about because it's ATMOSPHERIC here.

Yet, here we are. It's been more than a couple of weeks. No end in sight. He's played over eight, nine, ten plus HOURS straight. I try to be a good sport, really. I've played a couple games (terribly) but after the first week, his skills became so advanced that now I am merely "invited" over to watch him play. No more chatting in coffee shops, no more drinks on the hill, no more.... sex. It's gone. If I happen to bump into Mr. Guy during the day and ask him what he's doing that night, he says he has to "be somewhere."

That "somewhere" is in his living room playing "live" with all his other buddies with X-Box 360.

Oh wait, though, he's not ashamed of this affair. He strides in to tell me what new level he's made it with. How far and how much he can "score" with X Box 360.

His Facebook status is a reflection of how he's doing on X Box 360. If X Box 360 is being moody and he can't impress X Box 360 enough to get to the next level... well, he suddenly is "pondering the meaning of life." He got to the next level? His Facebook status is "life is awesome and everybody who doesn't savor every moment...." blah, blah, blah.

Look, mr. Guy. If you put even half the amount of time into ANYTHING else other than X Box 360 - you know those dreams you had about making it big? YOU'D BE THERE BY NOW!

I know there is no going back to the way we were before. I've seen it takeover the lives of my brothers, my brother's friends, Mr. Guy's friends.... I can't compete. It doesn't matter what lingerie I wear. This is the end. X Box 360 has worked her bitchy charms and you have fallen. I am only human, and apparently, so are you.

Application to be my Boyfriend

First, a little about me. I'm a 20-year-old good looking blonde attending University. I'm tired of wasting my time, so I have formulated some mandatory criteria in part A and part B is based on points.

Part A
1) You must be born male. I'll need to see a birth certificate.
2) You must own something to wear to a formal reception.
3) You must not own or ever wear Birkenstocks, Crocs footwear or randy river jeans.
4) All your parts need to be in good working order, further testing will need to be conducted of course.
5) I can't accept a regular drug user. Despite BC culture, I am including weed.
6) You must own at least four collared dress shirts. You need to look presentable standing next to me.
7) Your height must be proportional to your weight using the standard AMA guidelines.
8) You have to have lived in Victoria for at least two consecutive years.
9) You must have a photo which was taken in the last 3 months.
10) English must be your first language. Sorry, I'm not a part-time ESL teacher.

If you meet all of the requirements above then you may continue, if not, then you are now dismissed but thank you for applying to be my boyfriend.

Now: give yourself two points for each of the following criteria you meet

Part B

1) You have (or are working on) a post secondary degree.

2) You own a car and have a valid driver's license. Suspended for DUIs: minus 10 points.

3) You've never worn Ed Hardy, Affliction or any other Christian Audigier affiliated brand.

4) You follow at least one professional sport.

5) You have skills in bed. Not because you think you do, because your past experiences have told you.

6) You are not a born again Christian, Jehovah's Witness or any other kind of religious fanatic.

7) You have been to at least three countries outside of North America.

8) You don't need to call a handy man if something breaks around the house.

9) You know how to cook a meal for two.

10) You like stepping out of your bubble and trying new things like cuisine or bungee jumping.

11) You can make it through a romantic comedy without complaining (we don't have to tell your friends).

12) You have a great sense of humor. Are people laughing with you, or at you?

13) You can plan a good date without any help or advice from me. "I don't know, what I want to do" isn't an answer.

14) You work out and enjoy being physically active. I hit the gym regularly, you should too.

15) You have a job that requires more than a high school diploma.

16) You ride a motorcycle. I love to go riding.

17) You have a 5 year goal.

18) You aren't afraid of being yourself, even if you have a dorky side.

19) You're competitive, and I don't mean you like to battle it out with your WoW buddies on the weekends.

20) You know how to dance.

If you have a score of 30+ then please contact me immediately. If you scored between 20-30 pts, you can contact me, but I don't have a lot of hope for our future relationship. If you did not score high enough, then please do not contact me, but if at some time in the future you are able to improve yourself and meet the minimum requirements, then you may re-apply.

You MUST respond with your age (this is a creeper free zone, 20-26 year olds only please) and your picture.

I thank you in advance for your application; however, only successful candidates will receive a response.

Are you thinking about having kids? Teenager Kit!!!

Are you thinking about having kids? Don't want to go through nine months of agony just to have to go through it all over again if you want more than one kid. Well my friends, not only can I save you eighteen months of waiting, I can save years of diapers and unwanted stretch marks. For a limited time only, you can rent my teenagers buy one get one free for only $19.95.

Tired of your remote always being where you left it? Too much money in your wallet? Something not being broken and put back as if nothing even happened? Be the envy of all your friends with the only couch in the neighborhood to smell like Chinese food and dirty socks. Get rid of that needy feeling you had when your dog got hit by a car and had to be put down.

With my Teenager's Kit every day can be like a mystery. Will they come out of their room? Can the girl get off the phone in less than five hours? Will we go over our nine-hundred minutes on our cell phone plan?

Kids are old enough to work, but alas have no time. You must be able to pay for them to do whatever they want and their friends want or you are a bad parent.

Female teen is late four to five days out of the week and her school is halfway across town depending on where you live. This is largely due to hair and make-up not going on right and gets angry if you don't stop at Starbucks and drive fast enough. Games that are also fun, I need a ride and by the way can we pick up my friend's too? Followed by the classic and also my favorite, My friends have no ride home because…. You can play these games with the female teen all month long.*Caution: Female Incredible Hulk Game is good only seven days out of the month. Watch as her eyes become greener and her clothing becomes tighter. *WARNING* do not, I repeat do not comment on the tight clothing; the female teen will become angry. And you won't like her when she's angry!!!

Male teen can entertain for hours with games when you clean his room or look for missing dishes. I like to name these games; Find that dish. There's a fungus amongus, and even get the friends and family over to play. What's that smell? You may even have to guess if the boy is even home which is why I love the game. Will the boy wake up before five pm after playing W.O.W. on the computer all night? Another game to enjoy is deep thoughts by male teen including.

I should not have to do this because and best of all I don't have time to do this or I didn't have time to do that because... Do not anger the male teen by disagreeing, you may hear words that your mother would wash your mouth out with soap for. Let's not forget the mystical food fairy that comes during the night and leaves dishes and food all over the counters. If you have a pet, such as a dog or cat, don't worry they will help you clean such items by eating them and leaving wrappers on the floor.

So, if this is for you pull out the keys to the Mini-Van and empty the 401-K. (No-refunds, perverts, void where prohibited.)
Thanks,
[Deleted] A.K.A. Mom Slave
Please respond to tearingmyhairout@[deleted]

Sturdy chassis, lightly used (but highly driven) seeks new prospects.

Manufacture	Made in Atlanta, GA, 1968
Odometer	14,600 days
Hybrid Fuel Technology	pepperoni vegetarian
MPG (my preferred ground)	9% urban, 91% elsewhere
Audio System	one exceptional speaker, sensitive receiver, multiple frequency scan

STANDARD FEATURES

- hair conditioning
- "your turn" signals
- cat allergic converter
- self-starter
- vibram treads
- not much of an airbag
- rack and piñon
- minimum idle talk
- internal navigation
- love compartment

67 POINT PRE-OWNED CERTIFIED INSPECTION

- power staring fluid
- fool filter
- recognition switch
- pistons (and pissed offs)
- gimme a break fluid
- hair filter
- no power strain
- drama-free
- smoke-free
- drug-free
- disease-free

OPTIONAL PACKAGES

Off-Road Accessories

add-ons for exploring the outdoors— camping, snowshoeing, hiking, stargazing, photographing

Sub-Woofer

Complements the role of man's best friend with leash, extra water, nose printed windows, and scattered hair for added comfort. Wet dog scent additional charge.

MINIMUM DEMOGRAPHICS FOR SUCCESSFUL PROSPECTS

Physical	Y chromosome; over 5'7"; fit width of coach airline seat; 30's-40's
Cultural	adherence to strong moré / value system; interest in the arts, reading, travel, South Park; acting goofy/corny with kids AND adults
Economic	FT employed and/or financially stable
Intellectual	110% neurons firing; literate; creative; witty banter
Spiritual	Introspective and centered; disbelief that some guy 2000 years ago died for your sins.

Photo ID required with detailed application. All creative responses will be responded to in a timely manner. (Try to avoid the obvious hose, pump, and purring jokes.)

Since I have subsequently received a wide range of responses, please realize I made the effort to set myself apart from others, so try to do the same for yourself. And for those of you who are a tad jaded and have the impression that I'm soliciting something: (a) you're way off base; (b) click on that handy back button.

The First Annual, Only Moving Sale Ever #1! It's awesome, seriously.

*** Craigslist exclusive! Get this stuff before we set it up in a garage sale on Sunday! Or, e-mail us to get the location of the garage sale on Sunday! ***

We were going to call this the "Feast on our Dreams" moving sale, but that sounded too dire. We're going back to school, which means we're shedding household goods like nobody's business, except apparently for the lady next door! Feast on our dreams of glory! Buy some outstanding items! Many are on this rug! Some --- are not!

ITEMS FOR SALE:

1. **A Rockin' Good Stereo System** (3 CD changer, digital display, two speakers, black in colour, makes a lot of noise if dials turned fully clockwise):

As advertised above, it is both rockin' and good. We've got a new system, so we're leaving this one to the hounds. Caution to buyers: we turned the stereo on for this picture and Rod Stewart came on the radio. Actual customer experience may vary.

2. **A Tiny But Outstanding Microwave**: $40

Our new place comes with one, so the perfectly good old one goes on the market. We got it for $100 at The Brick when we had no stove, and we're passing the savings on to you! In the form of a microwave!

3. **A Three-Drawer Ikea... Thing**: $20

For more information, check absolutely any Craigslist furniture ad ever. (The girlfriend just told me the name is "Aneboda", which to me sounds more like a cousin of the cottonmouth snake than a dresser drawer, but now you can go online to find all the most up-to-date and relevant information pertaining to this set of three dresser drawers. Hint: it holds stuff in three compartments and largely looks like it does in the picture.)

(ADDITIONAL LATE-BREAKING MEMO: It appears that it sounds like I'm saying there are three dressers, instead of just one dresser with three drawers. THERE IS JUST ONE DRESSER. IT HAS THREE DRAWERS. LIKE IN THE PICTURE. STOP READING OVER MY SHOULDER. I AM DOING COMMERCE HERE.)

4. **K2 Rollerblades With No Brakes**: $10

Size 12! Slightly used! Is that gross? Probably! But IMAGINE THE SAVINGS! Non-warty former user.

5. **Big Empty Cloth Toolbox**: $10

For manly men (or women) who aren't afraid to say, "My toolbox doesn't clank!" And who among us has not had such dreams? Now those dreams can be realized, thanks to this awsome' great garage sale!

6. **A Big Stack of Empty CD Cases**: $ Free!

Are you a rock star? Was your last album rejected by purists? Have you flipped off a presenter at the Soul Train awards? Then this deal is for you! A stack of mis-matched empty CD cases are just the thing to boost your sales and audience perception of your incredible weirdness! (Alternatively, if you just have a band and want some CD cases to put your CDs in for sale at local shows, just come and... just get these things out of here. Please. You don't even have to be in a band. Although we could use your star power to draw more customers to the garage sale. So if you could tell others that you ARE a rock star and that you're coming to the moving sale, then that would be great. You can link to this ad from your MySpace page. That's all I'm saying.)

7. **A Ladder**: $15

Good for reducing the amount of low to the ground you are at any given moment.

8. A Fake Curled-Up Cat: $5

I am confident that if you were in an 8-bit adventure game you would really, really need this later on. Hedge your bets!

9. "Dread Pirate" Board Game: $10

Good for ages 8 and up! It's basically all luck, so even a dumb kid can win and go tell everyone at the party that he beat you and everyone laughs and wonders what the hell you're spending all that tuition money on.

10. "Trivial Pursuit" '70s Edition Board Game: $1

What could be more retro-chic than a board game where all the answers have to do with the USSR? In Soviet Russia, dollar buys YOU!

11. "Doodle Pix", Apparently?: $0.10

It can be yours for ten cents. Apparently we had this game all along. We are attempting to correct that situation.

12. Cuban Hexabox: $1

Is it a hexagon? Is it a box? Is it a humidor for cigar-like things that measure less than 3" in size? Why not all of the above! It's from friggin' Cuba, people! It's practically illicit --- at least at these prices! Zing!

13. CD Walkman: $5

All the versatility of an iPod with only one album on it, now 400% larger! If bigger is better, then you would have to be stupid not to be all over this deal! Could it be combined with the three vertical feet of empty CD cases to create the ultimate in portable entertainment?* I THINK SO!

* Actual entertainment not included

14. Planet Earth DVD Game: $10

Never used, but actually looks pretty awesome. We can't play it because she gets sad whenever she thinks about endangered species, so our crippling emotional problems can be your gain!

15. Wembly, Boober, Mokie and Gobo Driving Vegetables: $5

I'm sure these are collectibles worth $100 somehow to some person, so I'll discount 'em by the probability that anyone that gives two hoots is going to stop by the site. $95 seem like a pretty small discount comparatively? Brother, you ain't met Craigslist. (Edit: No, I do not know why they are driving vegetables.)

16. Pimp Brown Aldo Shoes: $10

Didn't fit. Whoops. Never worn outside the house --- size 11 or 12.

17. Dominoes: $0.50

Now in teal for the ladies!

18. Racquetball Racquet (never used): $10

Seriously, I'm going to go right down to that health club next Wednesday and sign up.

19. Guitar books: $ Free

Learnin' guitar is awesome and should be easier. Now it is, with these complicated books that no one can read since tablature and YouTube were invented!

20. A Big Red Binder Full of Secret Corporate Recipes: $5

That's right, everything from what's in the Big Mac sauce to how to make Red Lobster's delicious Diablo Shrimp. Wonderfully disturbing!

21. Door Chain: $1

The personal security device that says to burglars, "Hey! You're not coming in here! Unless you push, with your hand." Ineffective if applied to kitty doors.

22. Mice? Mouses? Meece? Mouses. : $0.50 each

23. Palm Pilots: $10 each

One comes with a leather case. It broke the other palm pilot's heart and took off with its sister on a motorcycle. It just doesn't care who it hurts.

24. Ethernet Hub: $5

Answers to "Charles".

25. Game Boy Advance and e-Reader: $30 for the GBA, $10 for the e-Reader.

Beats the best Amazon price by a week and five bucks. Also comes in a makeup bag, which I felt was pretty classy.

26. Phone: $5

Multi-function phone. Rings, dials, and takes both incoming AND gives outgoing calls. Cordless. All the convenience of a cell phone without the contract or pollutey satellites.

27. World's Most Awesome VCR with Remote: $10

We've had some good times, VCR. But now it's time for some other kid to enjoy editing MarioPaint cartoons of his very own. (Comes with programmable universal remote.)

28. Sproingy Clock: $5

I probably won't even sell this. It makes a HORRIBLE loud ticking noise that keeps my girlfriend awake and I just hide it all over the place so she thinks she's going crazy like in Telltale Heart. But she's making me sell it, so here it is. Avoid buying it and we'll see if in ten years I come home to find her scratching at the floorboards, fingers bloodied, hair matted, and with a look in her eye of a madness so profound that Mephisto himself could scarcely fathom a more scathing torment. Just five dollars!

29. Alarm Clock / AM/FM Radio: $10

Goes BLART BLART BLART. Alternatively, RADIO RADIO RADIO. Red numbers.

30. 300 Watt Power Source? $10

Pretty good price for a 300 watt power source. I can't remember if it's 300 or 400. It doesn't match the box. You'll have to e-mail me in order for me to muster up the energy to go look. I'm basically as lethargic as that raccoon over there.

31. Only Partially Busted Computer: $80, or best offer for components

I installed a new graphics card into this poor ol' girl without checking its power requirements. Aaaaaand the story comes together. :)
- 2.24 GHz Pentium 4 Processor (The 4 stands for "4get about it, it's awesome")
- Hard drive removed so's you can't hack my identity. Also protects copyright on all the stuff I wrote on there. And also any folders of a... private nature. You're on Craigslist, don't act like you're better than me.
- DVD-RW drive (8x?)
- 48x CD-ROM drive
- 2 gigs of DDR RAM
- 56k modem (awwww yeah)
- Either a 64 or 128 meg video card --- again, I'd have to tear 'er open to look.
- 10/100 Ethernet

- Inconspicuous tower casing belying the sheer awesomeness of the stuff within, excellent for spies or Jason Statham, who I think will be at the garage sale, you should come
- Probably a motherboard and 220W power source what done been fried up real good

32. What the hell, a stack of Darkhawk Comics? $20

Back in the spring of '02 I had a tentative deal with Marvel's Epic line to write a new Darkhawk series for the company. Then they fired Bill Jemas, cancelled the line, and I was left nude with nothing but a tea cozy and a pair of slippers (unrelated circumstances). At least you got the offer, you say? An invaluable experience, you muster? Hardly! I value it at precisely twenty of the dollars!

33. A CD Album: $5

All it lacks is an album cover.

34. A Framed, Matted Print of Picasso's "The Old Guitarist": $80

Celebrate the final years of Picasso's Blue Period with this proto-Cubist echo of el Greco. Covers up wall stains like a ***********!

35. Poubelle: $5

C'est une poubelle qui a une place ou on peut la frappe avec un pied pour l'ouvrir. On peut voir que tous mes livres francais ne sont pas en vente avec les livres au-dessous.

36. All Six Original Star Trek Movies: $10

Note: Star Trek II appears to have rocked its cover off. It might seem a bit shady, but I promise it's not a khaaaaan

* * * * * * * * * * * * *

Garage Sale Etiquette

Hello buyers and thank you for coming to our garage sale.

I know our newspaper ad and signs say that we open at 7 am, but if you arrive at 6:00, go ahead and ring the doorbell several times and peer into the windows until we answer. We'll open up early for you.

Feel free to show up with your unleashed dog, and of course, let him poop in the front yard. Our lawn-boy will clean that up later.

For your convenience, we've taken the time to mark everything with a price. But go ahead and keep asking, How much do you want for this?

In the mood for a cigarette? Come into the garage and light it on up. Grandpa doesn't mind if you blow the smoke right into his face. He's only on an oxygen tank. It's probably good for him anyway. And just leave the butts on the garage floor or flick them into the yard. We'll take care of those for you too. It's my mistake for not having an ashtray available.

And I know 25 cents is a fairly steep price. So let's haggle for 5 minutes about it. I don't have anything else to do today.

Also, pick up a bunch of items and then tell me what they remind you of. Be sure to tell me about every aspect of your life. Don't leave anything out. I'd love to hear all about you. And when you put the item back, just throw it in a completely different spot, upside down or just all wadded up.

Oh, and for some reason, yes, we did forget to put the hot water heater and the ladder hanging in the garage out on to the driveway so please ask us if we are selling it. Are you retarded?

Your McDonald's breakfast is going right through you, isn't it? Of course you can come in and use our bathroom. Be sure to look in the medicine cabinet for any prescription meds you might need. And there's some spray up in the window in case you drop a deuce. Hope everything comes out ok!

Wow, you want to buy all of our grandmother's antiques and at our full asking price? Oh, but you don't have any cash with you. Well yes, you can certainly write us a check and then drive off with the merchandise! No worries. I'm sure you're an honest person. Next time, we'll try to be prepared to accept credit and debit cards.

As you leave, be sure to rev up the engine several times, blast the salsa music and then lay a scratch as you drive away. It's loud, but oh so cool. Have a great day!

10 Reasons I Should Be Single/Celibate

1. Sex. what's the big deal? You like it, I like it. What we have here is a mutual trading of wants, some of that for some of this. Which, by the way, I'm told I'm quite good at. Is it because now that I want it you don't? I'm confused, didn't you used to like sex? I thought you did, and believe me, my libido hasn't diminished one ounce since I was 14. I'm tired of masturbating when you're around, what's the point? Sometimes you(I) just need to fuck.

2. Screaming kids. Hell no.

3. In-laws. Hell no. I barely tolerate my family.

4. My Body. Every married couple I know has become a chubby representation of themselves. Where is the skinny person I knew? I'm sure they're in there somewhere. My chances of not becoming a fatass plummet drastically when I get involved. I like working out, but when sitting on the couch cuddling becomes an activity, the gym forgets I even exist (or vice versa). Where has my waist gone?

5. My Brain. I was interested in learning once upon a time, I really was. I derailed my chances at grad school for a girl, a lying deceitful girl, and never looked back on my education. How do you revert my cerebellum into the primordial ooze it was millions of years ago with your sexy walk or whispering whiskey voice? What is this hold you have over me?

6. My Time. I like my free time: I can play video games, ski, go running, make coffee, play with the cats, shape the bonsai trees, clean the bathroom (it totally needs it!), and any of the hundred other activities I do when not involved with someone. Where does the time go when we chat and joke, filling my day with useless banter while the sun progresses across the horizon? I want it back. Note: Time spent in bed (a.k.a. #1) is hereby referred to as happy time, and not deducted from my potential free time. I appreciate that time, I really do.

7. My money. It seems like $100 bills fly out of my pocket when I'm

involved with you women. Where do they go? It used to be an easy trade, I would spend some money, then get some sex. Gone are the simple days of thinly veiled prostitution, where we get some food, have some drinks, then on to the fucking! Yes, I like the eating out as much as anyone, but our days and meeting up seem to revolve around food. Did I always eat this much? I remember when one good meal a day was sufficient. See #1 and & #4 for further clarification.

8. My friends. I used to have plenty of friends: ski buddies, drinking buddies, workout buddies, geek buddies, all around guy friends. Those have faded away over time, not really sure why, but I'll blame that on #1 too (Not my happy time, their happy time. Okay, sometimes my happy time too, like when I blow off my ski buddies to stay in bed with you). It's hard to make friends when you're older, mostly because they're a package deal: Ken and Trina, Neal and Heather, Mark and Stephanie. My friends aren't some amorphous blob that used to be two distinct individuals, but the changeling they've evolved into has only one thought process, as if they share one brain. I want my friend back! What possible wedge can I drive between them, since she is clearly providing #1? I have no weapon in my arsenal that comes close.

9. My Bad Habits. Heavy smoking, heavy drinking, copious amounts of drugs, porn, my slutty behavior, picking my nose, blah blah blah. You're tired of it all, I get it. Confronting me about it will only drive me to perform said behavior like a sneak-thief. Why do I feel guilty? No, I won't change, although I may slow down for the benefit of my liver. It told me the other day that he didn't sign up for this abuse, and he's moving on. He doesn't trust my random bouts of sobriety either.

10. My Sanity. Why oh why do I attempt to figure you out, damnable women? I'm sure in your brain that your behavior makes sense, but I bash my head in repeatedly attempting to figure you out. Please don't be cute and subtle, be direct. That's the only thing I understand, really, because underneath all of this, I'm just a big dumb animal.

I guess underneath it all, I am too concerned about the little (I shouldn't call him that) prick between my legs. He's gotten me into way too much trouble over the years. How does the lack of blood flow to my larger brain become disrupted? The only conciliation is that once I ejaculate (from #1, not from a manual override), I come back to my senses for a good 20 minutes, so feel free to ask me questions during that period. I might even be honest.

A personal ad.. in graph form

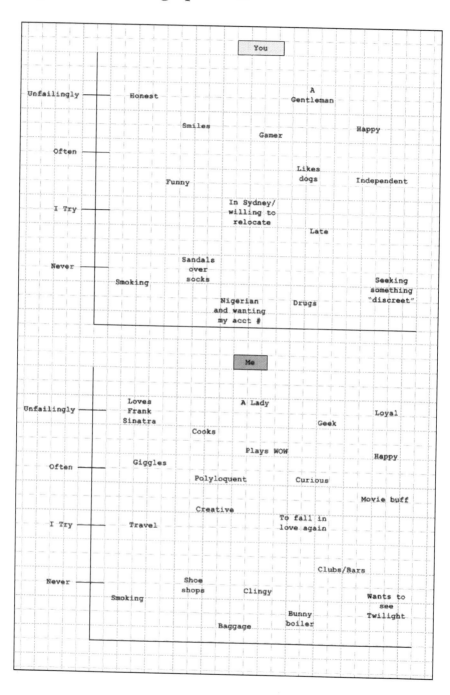

Magic wand to solve life's problems

If anyone has a magic wand that will solve all the problems in life, I'm interested in looking at it or buying it from you.

Would be interested in seeing the wand's past accomplishments and achievements to verify that it actually does what its supposed to. May request a demonstration. Prefer a fast acting wand, one of the later models that come with the instant gratification package or enhancements. If it isn't the instant gratification type, preferably one that lets you know whether or not anything's happening and gives a forecast of what's happening after waving it.

If it's portable that would be great, especially if it's pocket sized.

Color, is not important.

Prefer machine washable in case I forget to take it out of my pockets in the laundry.

Larger sized wands have to be storable in my apartment but am able to work around the size issue.

Prefer to have instruction manual if you still have it.

Am able to drive anywhere to pick it up.

Submit picture if possible!

Thanks.

Oh, and if you have a magic lamp instead that you need to be relieved of that still has wishes, I'm interested in that as well.

Thanks!

It isn't easy being a fat chick

Some observations from a 43 year old 5 foot 4 230 lb woman....

I have been working really hard at changing my life. I am down 35 lbs, up probably 10 in muscle. The first thing to vanish was my boobs and the last thing will be my frickin' belly. I feel much better, my eyes are clear, my clothes are all too baggy and fried food bothers my stomach. I also, for the first time in my life, find obese people upsetting and almost disgusting. This bugs me, it is hypocritical at best, I am still a fat chick!

Here are a few things I have noticed so far -

1. Most men still think me vulgar and ugly, never mind my pretty face and personality. But now, I am starting to see men at the gym doing one of two things - they either speak to me because I have somehow managed to be a gym rat in their eyes or they are starting to pay attention and be nice to me because they think that by some miracle I will screw them once I lose a bunch more weight, granted, this is my instinct speaking, I could be totally wrong. Either way, anyone who wasn't man enough for me as a really fat chick surely will not be man enough for me in the future, it kind of pisses me off.

2. 35 lbs is A LOT of fat. Next time you go to the grocery store, take a look at packages of hamburger in 1 or 2 pounds. Add it up, it seems massive. It feels that way too. Who knew that 6 months ago when walking on the treadmill hurt my feet so bad I could hardly walk that now I am biking and running.

3. Women are for the most part, negative about my success. Disguised as some sort of twisted cheering me on, most have something negative hidden in everything they say. WTF is that? Women truly are insane!

4. Trainers are useless to me! Most of them are just slick salesmen

who studied one book and took some test (not all, but this has been my impression and I have made it my business to get to know them all). The nicest people I have interacted with have been the biggest, baddest, buffest dudes and the most ripped ladies. Somehow they can see beyond the obvious and pick up on the fact that I am absolutely driven and determined. Some of them have been instrumental in proper form, putting together a solid work out and how to make a program work.

5. Chicks that wear a bunch of makeup and wear their hair down at the gym looking super hot are THE MOST SUPERFICIAL creatures walking the planet, AND they are dumb as rocks. What a waste of such beauty.

6. Building muscle and losing fat hide themselves and manifest themselves in the strangest of ways. I plateaued at 35 lbs a month ago and yet people who haven't seen me in a month are still going "WOW you are losing weight!". So don't get so down when you hit one, your body is just adjusting, it is natural and a part of the whole deal.

7. It SUCKS being the fat one at the gym, it is not easy to walk into a place of sculpted beauties looking so pitiful. You have to absolutely dismiss all of those feelings and it is not easy!

8. Gay guys absolutely hate fat women at the gym, it makes no sense to me but they have mad attitude.

9. There is so much to learn, un-learn in bad habits and re-learn in good ones. Give yourself a break, you didn't get fat overnight, its not going away overnight. You have to stick with it, invest time and time pays off.

10. Young guys are much nicer than the young ladies.

11. Don't be a chicken! People bigger than you feel just as awful and awkward as you do, dare to share your enthusiasm with them, it really does help.

12. I hate brown rice and oatmeal, but they are my friends.

13. If you are gonna eat carbs, get your ass on the cardio machines and use them!

14. Elliptical machines are supposed to be easy on the knees, what bullshit! They are also usually made for people 5 feet 5 inches or taller.

15. Don't freak out when you build muscle in your upper body and your bras get tight! Build enough muscle and the fat will start to fade, it will pass.

16. 6 meals a day really is a great ticket, eat protein with each and every one of them.

17. If you are really working the weights, start incorporating a protein shake of some sort immediately after your work out - if you wait more than 20-30 minutes your muscles will try and eat themselves.

18. One word - DERMAFINE-MD. It WORKS just as well and is much cheaper than Strivectin.

19. Please for the love of all things sacred, lose weight for YOURSELF. Forget the porn/media driven body image and trying to be something for someone else. You MUST strive above all to do it for YOU (everyone else gets a bonus when YOU succeed).

20. COUNT EACH AND EVERY CALORIE AND MAKE THEM COUNT. If you don't eat enough, your body will eat your muscles, if you eat too much and the wrong type, back comes fat.

21. YEP - that guy you absolutely could not believe was looking at your hoochie when you were doing leg presses really was. Nope, he doesn't want to screw you but somehow can't look at you.

22. YEP - that awful bimbo who looks at you with such disgust really does think you a loser, fuck her and the sugar daddy who

bought her those boobs.

Well I am rambling, I just wanted to share a little of what I have learned and seen. I hope it helps someone out there. You really can be successful, just remember that courage is not the absence of fear but the judgment that something else is more important than fear - YOU!

Allow me to complicate your semi-charmed life

So, you've got a great job, a house, a car. Your friends are encouraging and supportive. Your family adores you. Dogs, cats, and children flock to you.

But, you're just missing that little something. You just need a little more flavor. Something to keep you on your toes.

I've met your type before and I know just what you need.

I can provide you with a ration of anxiety attacks, sleep disturbances, and newfound paranoia. I am also willing to upset the most solid of friendships, anger your mother, and challenge your ability to keep your job. I can convince you that you are responsible for my well-being and, despite the havoc I leave in my wake, you will be inexplicably attracted to me.

I'm sure you're wondering how I will accomplish this feat. That is not important. My undeniable sex appeal, charm, and natural talent for mayhem will not fail.

What you should be asking is why. Why would you want this? Well, you'll be the first to admit that your comfortable life is getting quite dull. Once our courtship ensues you will have a renewed appreciation for the ho-hum. You'll catch glimpses of the life you once had...casual drinks after work, football on Sundays, barbeques in the summertime...and though you'll long for those days, you will feel wounded, crippled, unable to crawl back to that time. Eventually, though, I will feel you've had enough. I will leave you helpless, friendless, and so accustomed to my insatiable sex drive that you will continue to be isolated, frightened, and incapacitated in my absence. A ghost from your past life will find you, just before you turn to hard drugs to soothe your scarred psyche, and will nurse you back to emotional health.

This journey, this voyage will create a lifetime of unwavering appreciation for all of the things you had once thought to be dull. Food will taste better. Laughter will be more joyful. Warm human contact will be orgasmic. Plus, you will have an abundance of interesting stories to share with your loved ones. This experience may even lead to a new career as a motivational speaker.

Why am I willing to offer this life changing experience?

Well, frankly, I really need a good back rub right now.

Girlfriend Position Available

Objective:

To find a Girlfriend (between ages 25-35 with picture) who is deserving of my time, energy, and extensive experience.

Skills Looking For:

Good Humor (Likes a guy who is always funny)
Can Have An Intelligent Conversation
Great In Kitchen Doesn't Mind Cleaning
Porn Star Characteristics (Just Kidding)
Some Knowledge of Sports
Ability To Charm Parents
Wonderful with Children
Does Not Like To Shop & Drag Boyfriend Around
Can Ask Instead of Nag
Has Jealousy And Insecurity Issues Under Control
Ability To Get Along Great With Co-Workers Friends

About Your Co-Worker:

He is nearly 33 years old, 5' 9", Brown Hair, Green Eyes, answers to Sean. His hobbies are building houses(He has now built 3 of his own), higher education, has taken massage classes(For fun), likes anything funny, keeping in contact with his many lifelong friends, answering e-mails, and occasionally primping his hair.

About The Position:

This is a PART TIME opportunity to start. Hours are flexible. Full time hours may be available after satisfactory reviews by the advisory board. Applicant should live near the Sacramento area. There is an immediate need to fill this position this week. But offers will not be made to non-qualified applicants.

Individual must be willing and able to do the following:

-Articulate well on the phone and has sound communication skills.
-Must enjoy long sensual massages (For your co-worker is an expert)
-Is able to write "straight-forward" emails to staff. Sarcasm is not only appreciated, but is strongly encouraged.
-Must know how to have fun in a relaxed setting. We work hard, BUT play harder.
-Be somewhat athletic, and driven to succeed.
-Impulsive, yet sensible.

(Your co-worker has two part-time children from a previous marriage. Being a single mother is absolutely a turn on and brings conversations to a mutual level. Please apply.)

QUALIFIED POTENTIAL APPLICANTS SHOULD APPLY TO THIS POST IMMEDIATELY! Include picture if you have one.

Seeking Pretend Girlfriend

After reading ad after ad on Craig's List about individuals seeking to find a relationship offering meaning, contentment, or an opportunity to be spanked by a dominant transgender nun, I have decided that all I really want right now is a pretend relationship.

The benefits of a pretend relationship lie in being able to communicate (via email only) with another individual about things that are not actually occurring in one's life. It's the incredible chance to be completely dishonest with another individual who wants nothing more than a beautiful pretend connection with another soul.

We needn't share photos, real names, or accurate personal data. I will never ask you to call me, meet me, or send me your bank account routing number to help a deposed Nigerian dictator who will pay you back in millions. I just want to have a deep, intense relationship that has no actual roots in reality.

To be my pretend girlfriend, you must be exceedingly intelligent, articulate, and edgy. Your sense of humor must be phenomenal -- I would never pretend date someone who was not incredibly funny. You should be quite beautiful with striking features, (though I will never really know if it's true). It's essential that your mastery of English includes proper spelling. I will pretend break-up with you in a heartbeat if you make lots of typos. That's a major turn off...

I am (in truth, just this once) a really bright, very good looking physician, who is probably running a bit hippomanic in recent weeks. I am coming off of a very painful pretend-break up, so I might be pretend rebounding right now.

Don't Work? Won't Call? I might be the girl for you

Well, since I seem to have a very specific type, I'll just lay it out there.

I'm apparently really into the shiftless layabouts. If you are unemployed, unmotivated and possibly still live with your parents... you could be next in my long line of failed relationships! Just think of it... an educated woman to show you how things work (hey, I'm even handy around the house - you won't have to raise a finger!). A woman with drive, ambition and goals to contrast your utter lack of motivation. A girl with a thick skin who can roll with the punches and both dish out AND take jokes... I'll be happy to be the one who doesn't sugar-coat things so that you can blame ME for all of your hurt feelings and failures. It's probably even ALREADY my fault and you haven't even emailed me!

I am completely co-dependant, so you don't have to worry about me booting you to the curb over petty things (like finances, commitment or general civility). In fact, you could probably take my cash, sleep with another girl and then come over and break some things in my house and I'd just clean it up and continue along our path of destruction.

So if you're looking for a lady to use and abuse, I'm your girl! I have a house, a car, a life, friends, pets and my shit together. Please, I need some sort of zeitgeist in my life to screw all of this up! It's been way too long since I've been reminded of how awesome it is to be undervalued.

I'm over on minutes this month, otherwise I'd put my phone number up for you to call right away (either from your parents' landline or collect, from jail). So just email me and maybe we can work something out. Pick you up? Well, yeah, if you need me to!

Baltimore? No problem. It's only about an hour's drive. I don't mind one bit, I've got nothing but time!

WANTED: Husband

After too many trips to Home Depot and Lowe's it has become apparent to me that I need a husband. I am currently accepting applications.

Suitable candidates should be able to demonstrate proof of the following:

- ability to fix stuff around the house, car repair a major plus
- can lift heavy objects without complaining
- can offer an opinion on home decorations (but not too vociferously should they differ from my own)
- ability to get lid off tough jars/cans of paint/other packaging
- ability to carry stuff for me where necessary
- high boredom threshold re. multiple trips to Lowe's and Home Depot
- high performing "man parts"

Ability to carry out minor plumbing and electrical projects, hold a conversation on a variety of topics, some level of social skills, emotional maturity, creativity, interest in culture/politics etc and financial solvency are a plus but not essential. Well, on that last point... I do want a boob job and can't really afford one.

Bonus points for: ownership of power tools (and knowledge of how to use them) and suitable transport for necessary purchases.

What you will get is a wife who fits the following description:
- brown hair and eyes, average height, curvy figure
- no kids, no drama
- relatively intelligent/interesting/attractive
- considered to have a somewhat dry sense of humor
- raised in the south and has good southern manners

- can take me to meet your mom/boss/friends without embarrassment
- loves sex and will put you to the test to keep up with her

Please send applications including full relationship history, previous 'fixing stuff' experience, salary details, your social security number, your mother's maiden name, full medical history, five references, your inside leg measurement and shoe size to the CL email address above.

Preliminary interviews will be held in the coming weeks and may include a practical exercise.

Previous applicants need not apply.

Girlfriend Potential Test

Instructions: Please answer the questions below as directed in each section. You will be marked for grammar, spelling, cleverness, creativity and boob-size. Please keep in mind that while this is not an application for a job, your performance on this test will be a reflection of your ability to achieve certain positions once out in the real world. When the clock strikes the hour, you may begin. You have sixty minutes to complete the test.

Section One: Multiple Choice (Answer All, 5 points)

When submitting answers via email, please copy and paste the question and then your answer selection beside it.

Q1. Six months into our relationship, I go away to a tropical location with my family for a week over Christmas. This vacation was planned as a family event two years prior to meeting you. This is:
a) A great opportunity to get some things done without me around.
b) A great opportunity to attempt to sleep with my college roommate and/or my boss.
c) A sign that you are probably just a casual thing that I could toss aside at any given moment despite the fact I bought you probably the most thoughtful gift you've ever received and written you a letter for every day that I'll be gone, inciting you to 'Go on the Defensive.'
d) Occasion to have a sexy dinner at home the night before I leave, and a mini 'welcome home' party when I get back that's guest list is just you, me, a bottle of wine and a pack of condoms.

Q2. We've talked every night for eight days (not including the dinner/opera show I took you to on Saturday night that was followed by possibly your worst performance in bed ever, or the Monday night that I came over and we spent the evening making Rachel Ray recipes and watching Heroes followed by the best oral sex I've ever given you), with conversation time averaging about an hour per night. On a Thursday night, when on a deadline, I express a need to get off the phone so I can finish some work and go to bed at a reasonable hour. You:

a) Express your feelings of devotion in three words or less, then and quickly say goodbye after confirming plans for tomorrow night are still on.

b) Say goodbye, but then immediately begin talking about something that we hadn't discussed as thoroughly as is scientifically, legally or religiously possible two nights prior.

c) Take that as a sign that I'm abandoning you, and begin to point out that because of it I have commitment issues, that you're clearly not my priority, and then cry.

d) Say goodbye, but manage to do it with such menace and venom that I stay on the phone for another three silence filled hours, broken only by fits of gentle weeping and suicide threats.

Q3. I'm throwing change at your cleavage, which is readily on display in that loose fitting tank top you wear around my place on Sundays after brunch. Do you:

a) Wing the largest of the coins at my head, with an evil glare and then refuse to speak to me for the rest of the day.

b) Encourage my behavior, and allow me to purchase Afternoon Delights from you at discount prices.

c) Cry.

d) Cry and pick a fight with me, taking my actions as a total lack of respect for you and then begin to point out that because of it I have commitment issues, that you're clearly not my priority, and then cry some more.

Q4. We're having a fight. You:

a) Throw me out of your apartment, then thirty minutes later send 17 texts and attempt to call 13 times in the space of six minutes.

b) Give me space when the discussion gets too heated for rational thought, and redress your complaints in a calm manner when we've both had a chance to cool down.

c) Flip me the bird.

d) Wail on my junk.

e) both c and d

f) realize that the fight is about nothing, and begin creating fictional problems and make wild accusations about my obsession with material goods and having a wandering eye.

g) f, then d, then c.

Q5. I play [video games OR tabletop gaming OR fantasy football]. You:

a) Want to join in, because it looks like hella fun.

b) Leave me to it, in the hopes that I'll leave you a few things to participate in on your own.

c) Attempt to get me to quit, and use tactics like nagging, vandalism and emotional sabotage as an effective campaign against what you call my 'nerdy addiction.'

d) c, but also include deriding me to your friends.

Section Two: True or False (Answer All, 10 points)

When submitting answers via email, please copy and paste the question and then your answer selection beside it.

Q1. Rationale and Reason are the same thing.

Q2. A cheerleader AND/OR schoolgirl outfit is a wardrobe must.

Q3. Talking in your 'cute voice' just before you put my balls in my mouth is sexy.

Q4. Learning body language and communication cues is important.

Q5. 'Anchorman' and 'Superbad' are hilarious movies.

Q6. "But it's cute when I do it" should be a legally viable defense.

Q7. Chest hair is gross.

Q8. Bono is probably the most important political figure of our generation.

Q9. Sex is an important part of a relationship, and should be had frequently, often, whenever possible - within moderation, of course.

Q10. A relationship is metaphorically a two way street. So is your butt.

Section Three: Short Essay. (Answer ONE, 5 points)

Please select one of the following questions and answer it as fully as time will allow. Please try and be as descriptive as possible, and where applicable, come up with at least TWO convincing arguments to support your case. Arguments must be backed up with cited evidence, not anecdotal perspective.

Q1. If I was a crime-fighting vigilante by night, what efforts would you make to support my cause about the rising threat of evil in this city?

Q2. Please come up with a convincing game-plan for having me come shopping with you, keeping in mind my retail oriented attention span is about twelve minutes, and I am prone to wandering after flashing lights and shiny things.

Q3. Please argue why you are (do) or are not (do not): 'Down to Earth', 'Have a sense of humor' and 'Laid back'. Bonus if you can include evidence to confirm that you truly do avoid 'head games.'

Please submit answers via the email link provided. Please also keep a copy of this test and your answers to submit to future suitors for reference. Remember to ensure your name, number and bra size are clearly written at the top of your paper, and don't forget to attach a photo (3/4 length or full).

Fun Facts

Can you cut a cake into 8 pieces with three movements?
Yes. Two vertical and one horizontal cut is all you need.

***

A clock that doesn't work still gives the right time twice per day.

***

Experience is a tough teacher. You get the test first.
Then you learn the lesson.

***

What is something the dead eat but if the livings eat it, they die?
Nothing.

***

Did you know that 1 in 20 people have an extra rib?

***

If you hear 3-2-1 at Kennedy Space Center it might not be a
countdown to a space shuttle launch. It is also their area code.

***

In 1865, the U.S. Secret Service was established to combat money
counterfeiting. Not protecting presidents.

***

The name Wendy was made up for the book "Peter Pan." It didn't
exist before the book.

***

Cinderella is known as Rashin Coatie in Scotland, Zezolla in Italy, and Yeh-hsien in China.

***

Around 40% of the U.S. paper currency in circulation was counterfeit by the end of the Civil War.

***

Percentage of American men who say they would marry the same woman if they had it to do all over again is about 75%.

***

The typical lead pencil can draw a line that is thirty five miles long.

***

Before air conditioning was invented, white cotton slipcovers were put on furniture to keep the air cool.

***

Births went up 46% in Texas after the invention of the air conditioner.

***

It costs about 4 cents to make a $1 bill in the United States.

***

It takes over 200 apples to match the vitamin C in just 12oz. of Broccoli.

***

Dipsomania means an insatiable craving for alcoholic beverages. More people in China speak English than all Americans combined.

***

The more things change. The more they stay insane.

***

All the planets around our sun rotate counter clockwise except for Venus.

***

The most dangerous job in the United States is that of a fisherman.

***

The USA bought Alaska from Russia for 2 cents an acre.

***

Did you know Walmart sells more apparel a year than all the other competing department stores combined.

***

Did you know? The Olympic was the sister ship of the Titanic, and she provided over twenty-five years of service.

***

The chances of making two holes-in-one in a round of golf are one in 67 million. But it's been done.

***

There are 628 roller coasters in North America thanks to the new With Wizarding World of Harry Potter at Islands of Adventure Florida.

***

If you know French you would know, Crayola means "Oily chalk."

***

It would take over twenty new mid-size cars to generate the same amount of pollution that a mid-size car would in 1960.

***

There are more stars in the universe than there are grains of sand on earth. I feel sorry for the guy in charge of counting them.

***

There are over one hundred billion galaxies with over a billion of stars each.

***

It takes over 25 cups of milk to make one pound of butter.

***

If your average you will laugh at least 15 times a day.

***

If you're in Spain, you're likely to pour chocolate milk on your cereal.

***

The palms of your hand and the bottoms of your feet will not tan. They won't grow hair either.

***

Would you have guest? Apples are part of the rose family.

***

Amazing fact. A single leach has 32 brains.

***

It only takes 15 minutes to die from Carbon Monoxide.

***

Vampire bat saliva is used to help stroke patients recover.

***

Over 51% of households in the U.S. are single women. Only 17 % are single men.

***

If you are a single woman 25 years or older you won't be happy to know that there are only 1 single man for every 11 of you.

***

More than half of the court cases in the United States courts involve automobiles.

***

When you hear that a barrel of petroleum's price went up, there are 42 gallons in that barrel.

***

Most spiders can go a year without food.

***

The world's biggest bug is the Goliath Beetle. It can grow to 4.5 inches long and can weigh up to 3.5 ounces.

***

Sean Odom was the first to publish an article in 1993 on Search Engine Optimization (SEO), which is the process of getting your website to show up at the top of Internet search engines for particular search terms. It is an exact science that changes frequently. Sean Odom publishes a book every year which becomes an instant bestseller because almost every large company in the U.S. and Canada preorder the book from Amazon or Barnes and Nobles.

***

Having your website appear on the first or second page of Google.com or Bing.com is the equivalent of having a full page ad in every phone book in America 10 years ago.

***

The average flush of a household toilet uses 4 gallons of water.

***

You can waste up to 4 gallons of water a minute if you leave the water running in the sink.

***

The Papal Swiss Guard in the Vatican was founded in 1506 and is the only Swiss Guard that still exists. It guards the Vatican.

***

More than half of the coastline of the entire United States is in Alaska.

***

The Amazon rain forest produces more than 20% the world's oxygen

supply.

***

The Amazon River pushes so much water in to the Atlantic Ocean that, more than one hundred miles at sea off the mouth of the river, one can dip fresh water out of the ocean.

***

The volume of water
in the Amazon River is greater than the next eight largest rivers in
the world combined and three times the flow of all rivers in the
United States .

***

Antarctica is the only land on our planet that is not owned by any
country.

***

Ninety percent of the world's ice covers Antarctica . This
ice also represents seventy percent of all the fresh water in the
world.

***

As strange as it sounds, however, Antarctica is essentially a
desert. The average yearly total precipitation is about two inches.

***

Antarctica is the driest place on the planet, with an absolute
humidity lower than the Gobi desert.

***

Brazil got its name from the nut, not the other way around.

***

Canada has more lakes than the rest of the world combined.

***

Canada is an Indian word meaning " Big Village ."

***

Next to Warsaw , Chicago has the largest Polish population in the
world.

***

Woodward Avenue in Detroit, Michigan, carries the designation M-
1, so
named because it was the first paved road anywhere.

***

Damascus, Syria, was flourishing a couple of thousand years before
Rome was founded in 753 BC, making it the oldest continuously
inhabited city in existence.

***

Istanbul, Turkey, is the only city in the world located on two
continents.

***

Los Angeles's full name is El Pueblo de Nuestra Senora la Reina de
Los Angelesde Porciuncula -- and can be abbreviated to 3.63% of
its
size: "L.A".

***

The term "The Big Apple" was coined by touring jazz musicians of
the
1930s who used the slang expression "apple" for any town or city.
Therefore, to play New York City is to play the big time,

***

There are more Irish in New York City than in
Dublin, Ireland; more Italians in New York City than in Rome; and
more Jews in New York City than in Tel Aviv, Israel.

***

There are no natural lakes in the state of Ohio , everyone is
manmade.

***

The smallest island with country status is Pitcairn in Polynesia , at just 1.75 sq. Miles/4,53 sq. Km.

***

The first city to reach a population of 1 million people was Rome, Italy in 133 B.C. There is a city called Rome on every continent.

***

Siberia contains more than 25% of the world's forests.

***

The actual smallest sovereign entity in the world is the Sovereign Military Order of Malta (S.M.O.M.). It is located in the city of Rome, Italy, has an area of two tennis courts, and as of 2001 has a population of 80, 20 less people than the Vatican. It is a sovereign entity under international law, just as the Vatican is.

***

In the Sahara Desert , there is a town named Tidikelt, which did not receive a drop of rain for ten years. Technically though, the driest place on Earth is in the valleys of the Antarctic near Ross Island . There has been no rainfall there for two million years.

***

Spain literally means 'the land of rabbits.'

***

St. Paul, Minnesota , was originally called Pig's Eye after a man named Pierre "Pig's Eye" Parrant who set up the first business there.

***

Chances that a road is unpaved in the USA : 1%, in Canada : 75%

***

The deepest hole ever made in the world is in Texas . It is as deep
as 20 empire state buildings but only 3 inches wide.

***

The Eisenhower interstate system requires that one-mile in every
five

must be straight. These straight sections are usable as airstrips in
times of war or other emergencies.

***

The water of Angel Falls (the World's highest) in Venezuela drops
3,212 feet (979 meters). They are 15 times higher than Niagara Falls
.

***

I have always said you should learn something new every day.
Unfortunately, many of us are at that age where what we learn
today,

we forget tomorrow.

***

Made in the USA
Lexington, KY
10 December 2010